PROPOSALS AND CONTRACTS
FOR LIBRARY AUTOMATION:

GUIDELINES FOR PREPARING RFPs

By   Edwin M. Cortez

PACIFIC INFORMATION, STUDIO CITY, CALIFORNIA
AMERICAN LIBRARY ASSOCIATION, CHICAGO AND LONDON

1987

Published in the United States of America
by Pacific Information Incorporated
11684 Ventura Boulevard, Studio City, California 91604, and
American Library Association Publishing Services
50 East Huron Street, Chicago, Illinois 60611

This book is sold with the understanding that neither the author nor the publisher is engaged in rendering legal advice. If legal advice is required, the services of an attorney should be sought.

Library of Congress Cataloging-in-Publication Data

Cortez, Edwin M.
    Proposals and contracts for library automation.

    Bibliography: p.
    Includes index.
    1. Libraries--Automation--Contracts and specifications--Handbooks, manuals, etc. I. Title.
Z678.9.C637   1986   027'.0068'7   86-30664
ISBN 0-913203-17-3
ISBN 0-8389-2043-8 (American Library Association)

CONTENTS

FIGURES

Acknowledgements

Grateful acknowledgement is made to the following libraries and library systems for their cooperation in providing examples and sample text.

Ann Arbor Public Library
Chicago Public Library
Evergreen State College
Genessee District Library
King County (WA) Public Library

The author acknowledges Neal-Schuman Publishers for permission to print figures 3.3, 4.1, 4.2, 4.3, 4.4 and 4.5, which first appeared in *Managing Information Systems and Technologies* by Edwin M. Cortez and Edward John Kazlauskas (New York, Neal-Schuman, 1986).

Special thanks is also conveyed to Vendi Elman for the cover design.

Preface

Requests for Proposals and Contracts for Library Automation: Guidelines for Evaluation and Preparation is designed for librarians, information managers, consultants, and students. It describes how to draft and evaluate RFP's and contracts for library automation, as well as how to negotiate with library automation vendors. In tandem with its discussion of how to prepare procurement documents is a review of the basic principles of library automation and project management. The reader is walked through the various steps of managment practices such as conducting a needs assessment, preparing cost analysis, selecting staff and allocating resources for a library automation project.

Each of the five chapters in *Requests for Proposals and Contracts for Library Automation* describes one or more components of the procurement process for library automation. Chapter One establishes a perspective for library automation and includes a discussion of the library automation marketplace and of the state-of-the-art for automated library systems. It provides a foundation for the reader by surveying the functions of automated library systems and outlining the systems procurement process. Selecting candidate automated library systems, reviewing vendor proposals, and an introduction to the purchase contract are covered in Chapter Two. The use of staff and consultants in preparing the RFP and contract are reviewed in Chapter

5

Three. In this chapter a case study approach for drafting the procurement documents is presented.

Chapter Four is concerned with evaluating vendors for final selection, implementation and acceptance testing. This chapter also demonstrates the use of a variety of tools and techniques important for effective evaluation and testing. The final Chapter reviews in detail the content of the library automation purchase contract and how to negotiate it. The Chapter concludes with a discussion of on-going management activities after the automated library system has been implemented. Particular attention is given to the various phases of the library automation life-cycle and how best to control them.

Requests for Proposals and Contracts for Library Automation is intended to provide guidelines for drafting and evaluating procurement documents that accompany the acquisition of automated library systems. Actual phrasing and structure of the RFP and contract are included and can be considered for inclusion in the library's own RFP or contract. Although the nature of automated library systems is always changing, the practices for their selection, evaluation and implementation remain ever-constant.

Chapter One

PERSPECTIVES FOR LIBRARY AUTOMATION

Overview
General Procurement Practices
Project Management
System Selection Process

OVERVIEW

The growing options for library automation, coupled with increasing technological advancements, have made the process for acquiring automated library systems complex and replete with legal and quasi-legal considerations. The early technical support systems for libraries, from an administrative point of view, where acquired with relative ease. With the proper monetary appropriations in hand and a general list of system requirements, the library administrator quickly could identify, within the marketplace, the automated system able to satisfy the library's needs. This simple process was a function of the small library automation marketplace and the low level of sophistication at which these systems worked. A large amount of technical knowledge of

7

hardware and software on the part of the library administrator was unnecessary because options for either were few and selection was based on what was available.

As the marketplace expanded, new levels of sophistication for automated library systems were introduced. Technical knowledge of these systems became a prerequisite for effective selection. While applications on mainframe computers advanced rapidly from batch to online processing, developments in hardware facilitated the ascendency of the minicomputer for in-house dedicated applications. Further developments in hardware and telecommunications introduced the microcomputer for library applications, where, in a distributed-computing environment, these systems would emulate the power and sophistication of the larger minicomputer. Together these advancements increased the choices available for automating the library, and each choice increased the complexity of the process for identifying and contracting with the system vendors. In recent years this process has become more streamlined and detailed as the competition within the marketplace has expanded.

The large proportion of the library automation vendors operate in a vertical market. Each of their systems, for the most part, has evolved from a single applications approach to the current theme of the intergrated system. The prevailing marketing strategy, therefore, is to offer systems which have the highest degree of integration and to expand the number of integrated applications. A fully integrated system generally would include applications for circulation, catalog maintenance, public access catalogs, acquisitions, serials, and administration. To date, only some of these applications have been integrated successfully into one system and made available to libraries.

The vast majority of these systems today is offered as turnkey packages to include the following components. Each of these components must be given detailed attendtion during the procurement process.

    o Functionality requirements of the automated library system

    o Technical requirements for the automated library system

    o Performance requirements for the automated library system

    o Maintenance requirements for the automated library system

o Costs requirements of the automated library system

Functional Requirements. During the 1980s, libraries have sought to acquire automated library systems which integrate the separate major functions of the library's operations--circulation, catalog maintenance, public access catalogs, acquisitions, serials, and reference. The degree to which these systems has been successful is beyond the scope of this chapter. However, in theory, the integrated automated library system provides control over the major functions through the use of a common bibliographic database. The automated circulation function provides control over borrowers, charges, renewals, discharges, blocks, holds, recalls, fines and fees, overdues, reserves, materials booking and interlibrary communication. The automated cataloging function allows for the loading and manipulation of MARC records and fields and the online conversion of newly acquired records. The public access catalog (PAC) provides direct access to users of the bibliographic records. The automated acquisitions function provides control over selection, entry and review, verification and searching, purchase order preparation, receiving, claims and cancellations, vendor records and fund accounting. The automated serials function provides control over ordering of subscriptions, vendor notice preparation, check-in, claims, cancellations, binding, routing and accounting. The automated reference function provides control through a multi-level system of authorization to perform inquiry. The inquiry function is facilitated by author, title and subject access. Inquiry is further facilitated through the use of Boolean operations.

Technical Requirements. Technical requirements can be separated into three areas: hardware, software and database contruction. Hardware requirements usually dictate that the library will acquire a state-of-the-art computer configuration with sufficient primary and secondary storage capability to meet the immediate and projected work load demands of the library. The computer configuration should have the capability for modular expansion to meet the long term growth needs of the library. The inherent requirement of the database management system and utility software is that they support the functional, technical and performance aspects of the automated library system. The programming language should meet industry-wide standards and be written in a manner which enables efficient maintenace and upgrading. It should have multitasking, error detection, database protection, and messaging capability. Database construction requirements mean that the automated library system will allow for the loading and maintenance of a number of related files that include borrower records, bibliographic records, transaction records, item records, authority records and other similar items. The automated library system should be capable of accepting and differentiating between MARC format types and accomodate all fields of the MARC II formats. The automated library system should be capable of interfacing with time-share systems for the purpose of down-loading bibliographic records and converting them to local standards.

Performance Requirements. Performance requirements mean that the functional, technical and cost requirements will be achieved as anticipated and documented by the library. Criteria for assessing performance will be applied through a variety of acceptance tests.

Maintenance Requirements. Maintenance requirements mean that the library automated system will receive on-going support through the issuance of new releases of software and training and through performance monitoring. Fixes to the software and hardware should occur in a timely manner. Costs for maintenance will be commensurate with services received.

Cost Requirements. Cost requirements can be viewed in two ways: First, that over time there will be reductions in what would otherwise be unavoidable cost increases. For example, additional acquisition of materials, without automation, could mean increased cost in such areas as circulation and handling overdues. Second, costs can be evaluated in terms of benefits. For example, increased flexibility for shifting resources to activities more in need of them; or added productivity of staff members.

GENERAL PROCUREMENT PRACTICES

Formal and systematic procurement practices should exist whenever an agency enters into a significant capital expense as, for example, with the purchase of a large-scale automated system. The need for a formal procurement process is particularly acute when there exist two or more distinct alternatives from which to choose.

As the largest consumer of capital equipment, the United States Government has, through long use and experience, impacted the major procurement practices used in both the public and private sector throughout the United States. These practices are discussed below in the context of acquiring library automation systems and services.

Request for Quotation. The Request for Quotation (RFQ) is a preliminary procurement document often used to solicit pricing information when the information is not readily available in the marketplace, or is difficult to determine because of the complexity of the automation project. The document contains an overview of automation requirements for hardware, software, installation and maintenance. As the major components to automation, cost estimates for each will provide a realistic "ball park" cost figure for the total project. Responses from the marketplace to the RFQ will enable the agency to determine the degree to which their major automation requirements can be achieved and whether or not they are affordable. The RFQ provides the authority to proceed with the project, and the opportunity to reconsider the requirements in a realistic manner.

Invitation for Bid. The Invitation for Bid (IFB) is a common procurement document used almost exclusively by local governments and at the Federal level. Unlike the RFQ, this document contains a detailed description of all automation requirements, including functional, technical, performance and costs. As the name implies the purpose of this document is to invite bidders to address the needs for automation within the context of costs to the agency. The objective is to identify the bidder(s) who can meet the minimum requirements for automation at the lowest cost. The procedure is highly restrictive, requiring the agency to enter into contract negotiation with the most competitive bidder. In the event that two or more bidders meet the minimum requirements at identical costs, the bidder that best exceeds the minimum requirements is the one with which the agency enters into contract negotiation. Any attempt by the agency to deviate from these procedures or change its requirements during the bid, invalidates the process and forces the agency to re-open the competition.

Request for Proposal. The Request for Proposal (RFP) is the most common procurement document used by libraries acquiring automated systems and services. As a document it is identical to the IFB and its purpose is also to identify the most competitive bidder(s) who will meet the minimum requirements at the least cost to the library. It deviates from the IFB procedure in that it is a negotiated bid process. Once the RFP has been written and offered in the marketplace, the library can negotiate aspects of the requirements with the bidder(s) who are most competitive and responsive to the library's needs for automation. Alterations to the RFP and the bidders response can be made in an attempt to identify the most cost-effective automated system for the library. The methods of RFP preparation and the negotiated bid process are topics discussed in Chapters 2 and 3.

Sole-Source Bid. The sole-source bid is a method used when there is only a single source for meeting the library's automation needs. The bid process is limited to one vendor or manufacturer because it is the only one that can demonstrate quantitatively its suitablity for the requirements of the automation project. The improbability of library automation requirements being unique or so specialized, however, reduces the chances that a sole-source procurement is ever appropriate for library automation. It never should be used to circumvent the process of the alternative procurement practices outlined previously or be used as a result of someone's subjective judgement that there is only one possible source for meeting the automation requirements of the library.

PROJECT MANAGEMENT

In order to avoid planning an automation project that is at difference with the library's central mission, goals for the project should be established at the outset. The purposes of the project goals are to outline the long-range automation plan, to identify project constraints, to provide justification for the project and to provide general evaluation criteria.

The goals, together with specific automation objectives, also guide the management of the project.

The responsibilities for project management include the following areas.

o Project planning and organization

o Identification of all staff, resources and outside individuals and agencies with which the project will interface

o Definition of all tasks--by the library and the automation vendor

o Development of budgets and schedules

o Monitoring and reporting

o Taking corrective actions

o Evaluation

Project Planning and Organization. Planning for the automation project begins with a review of the library's mission in the context of automation. This leads to the establishment of overall program goals and project objectives, along with a long-range strategy for automation. A draft document containing short- and long-term goals and project objectives should be circulated to staff and to the library's constituency for discussion and comments before the final automation plan is designed.

The automation project can be organized by function or by phases. Whichever method is used, planning must take into account the entire picture and make certain that each step is followed in a logical sequence, noting those steps that are dependent or independent from one another and which can co-occur.

The functional approach requires that all project activities be reviewed for their relatedness. Categories for similar activites then can be created for further consideration and implementation. The phase approach segments the total project into manageable units that are to be implemented a step at a time. This latter method works best with smaller automation projects that have limited staffing.

13

Staffing. Proper staffing is one of the most essential responsibilities of project management. At the most basic level decisions need to be made as to who will be involved, how, and when. These include library staff (clerical and professional), administrative and governing authorities, regulatory agencies and purchasing departments, computer personnel, vendors, consultants and attorneys, other libraries, telephone companies, library users as well as other agencies and persons.

The project manager or coordinator, as the individual with the greatest project responsibilites, should be selected with particular care. This individual in most cases should be a member of the permanent library staff who has wide knowledge of the library's overall operations. He or she should possess library automation skills, but above all have intimate understanding of the library functions that are to be automated. As a manager, the individual should have the trust and support from administration and be able to work effectively with peers and subordinates.

Definition of Tasks. It is the responsibilty of project management to identify clearly and accurately all project tasks. This is an activitity which requires coordination of data and project staff input. The most effective method of identifying tasks and reducing the possibility of overlooking any critical steps is the "walk-through"--a step-by-step examination and discussion by a steering committee of all the activities needed to meet the specific automation project objectives.

Budgeting and Scheduling. Projecting, allocating and controlling costs also are the responsibility of project management. Five-year cost projections are standard in procuring automated library systems. Costs are weighed against benefits, or inputs against outputs. When considering benefits, it is important that they be evaluated to ensure that true benefit is derived for each dollar spent, otherwise there is no justification for each expenditure. There are four categories of costs which must be considered in any projection: 1) direct costs, which are determined and applied directly toward the purchase and operation of the automated system; 2) indirect or allocated costs, termed overhead; 3) fixed costs, such as site preparation, capital for equipment, consultant salary, insurance; and 4) variable costs, which are propotional to the volume of work done by the system, for example, generating overdue notices. Distribution of automation funds follows a budget plan, using good accounting techniques to ensure that funds are expended as intended. Budget planning and control requires that an early and thorough assessment of all costs be performed, with particular attention being given to the less obtrusive costs, such as site preparation, record conversion, and implementation.

Any good automation plan includes, and should keep to, a strict schedule of events and activities. The schedule should be established against a time line and be set up to aid in identifying project milestones. A calendar of events is, perhaps, the simplest scheduling tool for an automation project. The tasks to be completed are listed with completion dates beside each task. The calendar can be detailed or can include only major events. Milestone activities easily can be identified through some notation, such as an asterisk.

Other scheduling methods include PERT and Gantt charts. The PERT (Program Evaluation and Review Technique) chart has the particular advantage of graphically displaying events that are dependent on one another, events which can occur indpendently, and events which can co-occur. In addition, the design of the PERT chart allows easy identification of milestones and critical paths, i.e., those events requiring the longest elapsed time for completion. The Gantt chart also is a graphic display of events according to some time line, (days, weeks, months), and is used as a helpful aid in observing events which overlap in time. These three scheduling techniques are demonstrated in Figures 1.1, 1.2 and 1.3.

Monitoring and Reporting. Monitoring the progress of the automation project and reporting progess to the library's administration are important aspects of project management. Progress always should be assessed in the context of the specific objectives outlined for the project. This assessment will enable the administration to evaluate the effectiveness of the project plan and allow for corrective actions, if necessary. Reporting should make use of formal and informal means through committee meetings, staff briefings, memos and reports. Effective reporting will result in a paper trail that documents the history and accomplishments of the project.

CALENDAR OF EVENTS

TASK	COMPLETION DATE
Writing the RFP	
Preparation of Introduction	1/15/87
Preparing the Technical Proposal	2/1/87
Outlining Special Requirements	3/1/87
Detailing System Specifications	3/15/87
Detailing Maintenance Issues	4/1/87
Preparing the Financial Proposal	5/1/87
Outlining the Contract Provisions	5/15/87
Type RFP	6/1/87

Figure 1.1

Calendar of Events

PERT CHART

```
        002_____    003_____    003_____    004_____
 _____  | Preparation      |   | Preparing the   |   | Outlining special |   | Detailing system |
|     | | of introduction  |   | technical proposal|   | requirements    |   | specifications   |
start |....>|                |....|                 |....|               |....|                  |>...
|_____| .  | 01-01-87/01-15-87|   | 01-15-87/02-01-87|   | 02-01-87/03-01-87|   | 03-01-87/03-15-87|  .
        .  |_____|   |_____|   |_____|   |_____|  .
        .                                                                                     .
        .                                                                                     .
        .          .............................................................             .
        .          .                                                                         .
        .        006_____    007_____    008_____    009_____   _____
        . | Detailing       |   | Preparing the   |   | Outlining contract|   | Type  RFP      |   |   |
        . | maintenance issues|....| financial proposal|....| provisions      |....|             |   |   |
        . |                |   |                 |   |                 |....|                  |...>| End |
        . | 03-15-87/04-01-87|   | 04-01-87/05-01-87|   | 05-01-76/05-15-87|   | 05-15-87/06-01-87| . |___|
        . |_____|   |_____|   |_____|   |_____| .
        .                                                                                     .
        .                                                                                     .
        .  001_____                                                                 .
        . | Project         |                                                                 .
        ..>| management      |>...............................................................
          | 01-01-87/06-01-87|
          |_____|
```

Figure 1.2

PERT Chart

17

GANTT CHART

TIME LINE (in weeks)
```
------------------------------------------------------------------------

                      Jan     Feb     Mar     Apr     May     Jun
                      01  15  01  15  01  15  01  15  01  15  01

------------------------------------------------------------------------

TASKS

Writing the RFP
001.  Project Management            x------------------------------x
002.  Preparation of Introduction   x---x
003.  Preparing the Technical Proposal   x---x
004.  Outlining Special Requirements       x--------x
005.  Detailing System Specifications          x---x
006.  Detailing Maintenance Issues                 x---x
007.  Preparing the Financial Proposal                 x--------x
008.  Outlining the Contract Provisions                    x---x
009.  Type RFP                                                x---x


------------------------------------------------------------------
```

Figure 1.3

Gantt Chart

Taking Corrective Actions. Any automation project will require management to make periodic assessements of the automation plan and its objectives. If the plan is failing to meet the project objectives, corrective action should be taken either to revise the plan or to modify the objectives. Modification of objectives only should be done if the library has established the priorities of the automation system. By knowing the priorities of the system, managment will be able to make the necessarily adjustments without violating the major requirements for automation.

Evaluation. Effective project management means that all aspects of the automation plan will be subject to constant review and evaluation. Methods for evaluating the automation plan have been discussed previously. In addition, however, project management also is responsible for evaluating expected and actual performance of the automated system. Construction and implementation of evaluation techniques is necessary to identify and select the automation system; to evaluate its performance prior to installation; and to evaluate and monitor its performance after installation.

SYSTEM SELECTION PROCESS

The process of selecting an automated library system requires a high degree of systematic and careful planning. The process should include the following aspects.

o Recognition and analysis of library goals and objectives

o Comprehensive needs assessment

o Costing for library automation

o Formal selection process

o Evaluation of alternatives and final selection

o Contracting for system and services

As pre-selection activities, the first three aspects of the process are discussed briefly below, while the remaining three are addressed in detail throughout the remainder of the book.

Goals and Objectives. Recognizing the library's overall goals is important in determining the specific objectives to be achieved by introducing automation. The systematic analysis of goals and objectives helps in specifying the requirements for automation and in evaluating the alternatives available.

Needs Assessement. The needs assessement study measures the difference between the library's actual state and target state: where it stands in relationship to where it would like to go. As a formal exercise, the needs assessment study reviews, with an eye toward automation, the operating efficiency of the library or a particular library operation, such as circulation. The process calls for identifying and examining a perceived problem within the context of the library or of an operation. Using standard research techniques for data collection and analysis, the needs assessment study should yield alternative solutions to the problem at hand. As an identified alternative, automation must be assessed carefully to determine the degree to which it resolves the problem and at what costs.

Costing for Library Automation. Costing is an activity which helps to quantify benefits in monentary terms. It is a decision-making technique used for evaluating and selecting from among alternatives. This procedure can be complex and should be executed with precision and thoroughness. The primary objective in carrying out a cost study is to increase benefits and to reduce cost. A by-product of a good cost-benefit study is the identification of the options which will be lost due to the decision to settle upon a particular alternative. For example, what opportunities will the library forfeit by purchasing an automated library system.

There are numerous costing techniques, the most vital for library automation is cost-benefit analysis (Cortez and Kazlauskas, 1986). In evaluating alternatives, cost-benefit analysis attempts to compare inputs (costs) and outputs (benefits) in monetary terms. The first problem encountered in such an analysis is the difficulty of expressing all outputs in monentary terms. For example, staff satisfaction and effects on morale are intangible factors. As such, every attempt should be made to factor them in by chararcterizing them as quantifiable elements. Assigning them an equivalent quantifiable weight at the time of final analysis is a method often used. Benefits usually are intangible factors and also are difficult to measure. The objective in considering benefits is to ascertain, as best as possible, the net cost value of individual benefits. The method requires careful consideration of which benefits can be translated into financial terms. For example, it may be necessary to determine whether a modem with a baud rate of 1200 is really needed if a 300 baud transmission rate will produce the desired results. Does it matter that online records from a bibliographic utility can be downloaded at a rate of 50 per hour using the faster transmission speed? The cost of the modem vs. the cost of a longer connect time to the bibliographic utility is what should come under analysis.

In calculating cost-benefit values all aspects of automation system procurement, from the needs assessment study to final installation and testing phase, must be considered. The objective is to determine the total cost. It is made up of a combination of fixed and variable costs, each of which may be partially direct and partially allocated.

REFERENCE

Cortez, Edwin M. and Kazlauskas, Edward J. *Managing Information Systems and Technologies.* NY: Neal-Schuman, 1986.

Chapter Two

THE PROCUREMENT PROCESS

Selecting Candidate Systems
Form and Content of the RFP
Reviewing Vendor Proposals
The Purchase Contract

SELECTING CANDIDATE SYSTEMS

The current marketplace for library automation (see Appendix A) with its abundance of stand-alone turnkey, microcomputer and distributed systems, offers to libraries a large and varied assortment of options for automation. As a result, the first step in procuring an automated library system is to narrow the options before final selection can be made.

In Chapter 1, the needs assessment study demonstrated how to identify alternative methods for solving problems or for meeting library requirements. Whether the alternatives include library automation or not, each class of alternatives may have many options, requiring still a further breakdown. The objective of an additional analysis, in the case of library automation, is to identify the candidate automated library systems that satisfy the major requirements of the library automation program. The major requirements are drawn from the library's automation goals. For example:

LIBRARY A:

The goal of the library is to acquire an integrated automated library system that will support the administrative, circulation, cataloging, acquisition and serial functions of the library.

LIBRARY B:

The goal of the library is to acquire an automated circulation control system that has the capability of modular expansion to meet the cataloging and acquisition functions of the library over time.

Given the divergence of major requirements of these two goals, one should expect the list of candidate systems for each library to be different. Of course, any system that met both of the library goals would appear in each of the two lists.

By analyzing the library automation goal in terms of its functional components, a candidate system selection matrix can be constructed for the purpose of identifying the major automated systems that potentially will satisfy the overall automation requirements of the library. Figure 2.1 demonstrates the technique. It should be observed that beyond functional requirements, the library may want to include other selection criteria for the candidate systems.

Having established a list of candidate systems, the library is left with a set of alternatives which meet the major requirements for automation identified in the needs assessment study and in the automation program goals. These alternatives should require more or less the same amount of inputs (costs) given the required outputs (benefits) for the automated library system. Final selection from among these alternatives is achieved by a formal selection process which includes an evaluation of the bids from responsive vendors.

Mandatory Function	Vendor A	Vendor B	Vendor C
Reserves	0	1	1
Reports	2	1	0
Boolean	2	1	1

0 = available

1 = not available

2 = in development

Figure 2.1

Candidate Selection Matrix

A formal procurement process is used to select from the various vendors and hardware/software manufacturers (here also referred to as vendors) who market library automated systems. Formal procurement is used by libraries or any organization that wants to be seen conducting business in an open and fair environment. The process allows for total evaluation of the candidate systems in order to select the "best qualified vendor", given the costs and requirements of the automated system. More importantly, because it is a competitive process, the vendor has a better opportunity to propose the best blend of computer equipment and service to support the needs of the library.

As mentioned in Chapter 1, the RFP is the technique used most often by libraries for advertised procurement. There are four major purposes to the RFP:

1) It is the sole formal document that makes known to the library automation vendors the specific needs and requirements of the library;

2) It serves as the primary template against which to evaluate the ability of the vendor to meet the library's automation requirements;

3) It identifies the level at which the library will accept the vendor's system and services;

4) It serves as the basis for negotiating a contract with the vendor.

In this chapter the content and format of the RFP is discussed. Chapter 3 will review its preparation using a case study approach.

FORMAT AND CONTENT OF THE RFP

The Introduction. An effective introduction to the RFP provides potential vendors with an explanation of the library's primary goal in acquiring an automated library system. More specifically, it provides perspective regarding how to satisfy the requirements of the library with the requested automated system. To this extent, the introductory passages should include: a succinct statement of the library's mission, goals and objectives; a detailed description of the library's organizational structure and governance; and a history of the library's development and current operations. Statistical information is appropriate in this section.

An overview of the content and organization of the RFP also should be provided. This should include a statement of purpose and requirements for the automated library system and a schedule of events concerning the distribution of the RFP (e.g., the various deadlines for responses, dates for evaluation of responses and contract negotiation, and dates for award of the contract). The introductory section should outline in detail the arrangement, content, and format of the vendor proposals. This will facilitate the unbiased evaluation of the proposal responses. Charts and diagrams, margins, headings, table of contents, references, equipment lists, glossaries, should be specified. It is often helpful to ask that pricing information be treated separately for easy reference and evaluation.

Additional instructions and information to the vendors may include procedures for submitting addendums and supplements to the RFP: a description of the library's proposal evaluation process; procedures for the withdrawal of proposals; procedures for vendor conferences; procedures for appeals and protests; and the means for contacting individuals within the library.

The RFP also should include the following information.

1. **Proposal guarantees** requiring that the vendor accompany the proposal with a monetary guarantee (usually 10% of the total contract), that states "if awarded the contract, the vendor will so execute or forfeit the proposal guarantee."

2. A **proposal-validity** period specifying the number of days the vendor will agree to maintain valid the proposal after submission.

3. A **payment schedule** devised in such a way that it places the burden of responsibility on the vendor for maintaining the delivery and installation schedule and other obligations covered in the contract.

4. Alternatively, a **performance bond**, which sometimes can substitute for the payment schedule, requires that the vendor place in trust a bond equal to 100 percent of the price of the automated library system, to be forfeited to the library in case a breach of contract. Many vendors will not respond to an RFP

which contains a performance bond clause because of the liability they might incur by tying up their capital flow.

5. A **warranty clause**, which itemizes all hardware, software, services covered, and specifies all warranty periods.

6. **Vendor obligations**, detailing vendor responsibility concerning delivery, installation, and maintenance.

7. An **indemnity clause**, which points to the vendor's contractual agreement to indemnify the library from and against all claims, damages, losses, and expenses arising out of, or resulting from the negligent acts of the vendor, the vendors employees, or subcontracts in the performance of the contract. (See Chapter 5, Negotiating the Purchase Contract).

8. A **starting date** specifying when work will commence after the contract is signed.

9. A description of the **performance test**, which will guarantee that the vendor has provided the technology to meet all the specified requirements at an acceptable level.

10. The type and level of **training** the vendor will provide with the automated system and the requirement that the vendor certify in writing that personnel have been trained adequately.

11. A **description of the documentation** to be provided with the automated system (manuals and system charts and diagrams) and to what degree the vendor will maintain this documentation as the system is upgraded.

Functional Specification. This second section is critical in the RFP. It specifies the activities the automated library system is expected to support and the products that the system should provide. The specifications should be grouped into "mandatory" and "desirable" categories, describing each function and its requirements in clear and understandable language. The functional specifications as a whole equal the operational components of the library's automation requirements. The methods for generating functional specifications are reviewed in Chapter 3.

Technical Specifications. Technical specifications are as critical as the functional specifications when preparing the RFP. Strategically, this section of the RFP should be approached from the point of view that it is the vendor who must specify, with exactness, the technical features of the automated library system. In detailing the technical specifications, the vendor must provide guidelines and minimum standards of the automated system, rather than merely defining the architectural features of either the software or the hardware components of the system. (See Chapter 4, Evaluation of Vendor Proposals).

An effective technical specification solicits from the vendor valuable information upon which to judge the degree to which the automated library system can meet the functional automation requirements of the library. The methods for generating technical specifications are reviewed in Chapter 3.

The RFP is a time-consuming document to write. There is, however, no need to design a completely original one because many RFP models are available. Written authorization to use part of another library's RFP is usually easy to acquire. Alternatively, vendors often have a file of RFPs from which appropriate ones may be selected. Obtaining advice from someone who has gone through the process always is helpful; there is no substitute for experience.

The RFP has the weaknesses of any bidding procedure. Primarily, it is difficult to write specifications that not only reflect a library's requirements, but at the same time exclude unqualified vendors from entering the bid process. Justifying why a bid is unresponsive is a difficult task, but can be avoided by preparing strict specifications from the start. There must be a balance against the tendency to overspecify, which many times leads to the ungratifying experience of receiving unresponsive bids. Many vendors complain that they are expected to respond to unrealistic specifications. As a consequence, they simply choose not to bid at all under such circumstances. Thus, in writing effective specifications, a good balance between what is air-tight and what is reasonable will help assure that only truly responsive proposals are submitted by the vendor.

REVIEWING VENDOR RESPONSES

Evaluation refers to the process of determining which vendors are deemed most responsive to the specifications and requirements as outlined in the RFP. Final selection, on the other hand, is the awarding of a purchase contract after a period of negotiation. Evaluation and final selection of an automated library system is the topic of Chapter 4.

In reviewing the vendor responses to the RFP, the technical sections of the proposals often are judged separately from the financial sections. The technical sections are judged on the adequacy with which the variety of the functional requirements and performance specifications outlined in the RFP are addressed. The financial sections are judged in the context of what is being offered against what can be afforded.

The review process begins with an identification of the vendors who are responsive in meeting the RFP's mandatory (functional and technical) specifications. The results of this initial review should be reported in a written document describing how vendors succeeded or failed to meet the mandatory specifications.

The next review phase begins to quantify the analysis of the remaining vendors by assessing the degree to which each meets the desired functional and technical specifications.

These initial reviews can be facilitated by using the candidate selection matrix (Figure 2.1). The criteria for selecting the candidate systems should be modified to be specifically relevant to the initial review process.

After determining the extent to which the vendors meet the desired specifications, those vendors who are proportionally under average in the number of desired elements included in their proposals can be eliminated from the bid process.

The remaining vendors are candidates for formal evaluation and final selection.

THE PURCHASE CONTRACT

The purchase contract for an automated library system is a complicated document to write and should be drafted by a lawyer. Negotiating the contract, however, is usually the responsibility of the library. Contract negotiation is the topic of Chapter 5. Special features of the purchase agreement or contract might include these categories.

1. **Clarification of terminology.** This effort is aimed at providing mutual understanding of the technical language used in the RFP to avoid ambiguity and to ensure complete understanding of the procuring agency's requirements.

2. **Maintenance documentation.** This provision requires that the vendor provide upon request, all diagrams, schematics, manuals, and other documents necessary for the maintenance of the equipment, usually at no extra charge to the library.

3. **Patent and copyright indemnification.** These features protect the library against claims of patent and copyright infringement on the equipment or associated documentation or software.

4. **Equipment condition warranties.** This provision ensures that equipment acquired under the contract is either newly manufactured from new or serviceable used parts, or is equivalent to such equipment in performance, reliability and durability.

5. **Software documentation.** The vendor agrees to provide appropriate software documentation, within a specified period of time, in a form mutually agreed upon.

Other contractual terms to be included may come directly from the RFP. For example: delivery and installation, acceptance test, conversion of data, performance bonds, training, warranties of vendor, payment schedules, installation schedules and penalties for non-performance. To ensure that other critical areas are not overlooked in the contract, the best alternative is to make the RFP a formal attachment to the contract.

No contract ever can ensure complete protection of the library. The best that can be hoped for is that as many contingencies as posssible have been considered and dealt with strategically in the contract. In the end, only good faith between the library and the vendor guarantees a fair, legal document protecting both their interests.

Chapter Three

PREPARING THE RFP

STAFF AND CONSULTANT RESPONSIBILITIES

Understanding and delineating staff roles for the purpose of drafting the RFP is an important management consideration. The question often asked is, should the responsibilities go to skilled library staff or to an outside consultant? The answer is to use both if financial resources permit.

Library Staff. The library's implementation team should consist of a project manager and representatives from the public and technical services areas of the library. This team brings to the RFP preparation phase a valuable history of the automation project and a familiarity with the automation requirements. As such, members of this team are in a good position to articulate these requirements in terms of system specifications. Staff can be assigned to draft the various parts of the RFP, then, in committee, integrate their work while checking the text for undesired redundancy and for consistency. As a committee effort the draft RFP is less likely to reflect personal biases and will achieve a higher degree of objectivity.

Consultants. There are a number of highly qualified library automation consultants available to assist in the preparation of the RFP. Their role, however, as advisors, is most cost-effective when used to validate the RFP and recommend wording for certain technical areas dealing with hardware, software and acceptance testing procedures.

There are three methods for identifying qualified consultants. The first and least recommended is to simply select a consultant from a list which can be obtained through the Library and Information Technology Association (LITA), or some other listing. The LITA list is an open list with names of individuals who have asked to be added as library automation consultants. Even if a name is a familiar one, there is no gurantee that this individual is the best qualified for your library automation program.

The second method is to obtain recommendations from libraries who have experienced similar automation projects and who have used consultants. These libraries can be identified through the various vendor user groups. It is suggested that three or four references be obtained for each potential consultant. One poor recommendation might be the result of internal politics in which the consultant played the scapegoat.

The third method is to issue an RFP for consultant services. This method is obviously more time consuming and expensive given the staff time necessary to draft the RFP, evaluate the consultant responses and make a final selection. It is, nevertheless, the most effective method for selecting a qualified consultant. The library's RFP for consulting services should include the following elements.

1. General rules and conditions for such items a submission of bids,

contract and delivery provisions, billing and payment requirements.

2. The scope of the contract identifying each major component of work being requested.

3. General background of the automation project including the library's goals and requirements for the automation.

4. Objectives for consulting services which identify the specific tasks that are to be performed, deliverables, meetings, reports and schedules.

The technical portion of the RFP should elicit from the consultant proposals the following information.

1. References of former clients.

2. A statement and discussion of the requirements as they are analyzed by the consultant.

3. The consultant's proposed definitive scope of work with explanation of the technical approaches to be taken and a detailed outline of the proposed program for executing the requirements of the consultant's work and for achieving the objectives of the project.

4. Preliminary layouts, sketches, diagrams and other graphic representations and other data as may be necessary for presentation or understanding of the proposed approaches and program.

5. A preliminary work plan that takes into account methodological issues, phases of the project, schedules and similar topics.

6. A statement of qualifications which includes organizational and staff experience and a resume.

In order to evaluate the viability of the consultants' proposed fee, the RFP should include a business section that elicits the following information.

1. The itemized cost for individual tasks and deliverables, including studies, reports and analyses.

2. A breakdown of direct labor and labor overhead costs, including hourly and daily rates, travel, per diem, clerical expenses and cost for equipment and supplies.

3. A summary of costs for all elements, tasks and components of the automation project for which the consultant will derive a fee.

It is always desirable to schedule an interview with the most competitive consultant(s) before the contract is awarded. The purpose of the interview is to clarify any questions or issues resulting from the consultant's proposal and to help determine the compatibility of the consultant to the staff and to the work that is to be performed. The interview is also useful for assessing the consultants ability to communicate with people, their knowledge of the field, and their professionalism, which includes the awareness that each library automation program has its distinct, local needs and that past experiences should not interfere with the creative commitment to meet the requirments of the automation project at hand.

DRAFTING THE RFP

The RFP is the library's primary vehicle for the procurement of automated library systems and services. As the process for acquiring an automated library system progresses, the library will become increasingly dependent on the RFP as a reference tool for understanding and evaluating vendor bids, and for monitoring time schedules and procurement strategies. As a reference tool one of the first considerations in preparing the RFP is a comprehensive "Table of Contents" to facilitate its use. Figure 3.1 is an example of a table of contents taken from an actual RFP.

Figure 3.1
Table of Contents for a Typical RFP

1.0	Introduction
1.1	Background Information
1.2	General Rules and Conditions for Submission
1.2.1	Overview of RFP
1.2.2	Schedule of Activities
1.2.3	Address of Contact Person
1.2.4	Date of Submission
1.3	Proposal Format
1.3.1	Arrangement
1.3.2	Number of Copies
1.3.3	Standardized Description of Development Status

The following sections of this chapter discuss each of the major content components found in a RFP. These include the introductory section, the informational section, the special requirements section, the system specifications section and the contract section.

THE INTRODUCTORY SECTION

Background Information

Background information is included in the RFP in order to give the vendors a perspective on the library's environment and general requirements for automation. The amount of background information will vary according to the type of library and the complexity of the particular automation project. The objective is to give as much information as possible that will be useful to the vendor in understanding the purpose, constraints and requirements of the automation program. Four examples are given on the following pages.

A Medium Size Public Library

The _____ includes a Main Library, three branch libraries, a bookmobile and several depository collections. Total holdings are approximately 360,000 volumes (including sound recordings) and 137,000 titles. Growth rate of library collections is approximately 7,000 titles and 22,000 volumes per year with projected average growth rate of 5% per annum. The library has 89,000 registered borrowers.

The library is governed by the Board of Education and serves a district-wide population of 125,000 residents in a 120 square mile area.

There are twenty-seven elementary and eight secondary school libraries plus an Instructional Media Center library. The library provides interloan service to school libraries. In addition, the library is a member of the _____ Library System, a cooperative of fifteen public libraries located throughout the region. The library interloans approximately 2,500 books annually to other member libraries within the cooperative.

A Large Academic Library

The University of _____ offers approximately 40 major fields of study through the Colleges of Arts and Letters, Science, Engineering, and Business Admnistration. On the post-baccalureate level, the Graduate School offers 28 courses of study leading to the master's degree and 21 leading to the doctorate.

Enrollment is over 9,000 students with some 7,000 undergraduates and 2,000 graduate and professional students. There are over 700 teaching and research faculty. The library staff consists of 34 library faculty, 89 FTE support staff, and 8 FTE student assistants.

The physical plant consists of nearly 100 buildings on 1,250 acres. The main library and seven campus libraries contain more than 1.5 million volumes and 680 thousand microform units, and subscribes to 13,000 serials.

The main library is the heart of the Libraries System containing the majority

40

of the collection, administration and centralized technical processing. It consists of a fourteen story tower, thirteen of which are designed as library space. Technical services is a the first floor and public services occupy the first and second floors. A fifteen hundred square foot room in the basement is being prepared as a computer room. The six branch library locations are within 2,500 feet of the main library.

The cataloged collection of the University Libraries System consists of 1.3 million volumes and about 750,000 titles. About 200,000 of these titles are on OCLC archival tapes and a total retrospective conversion project is underway utilizing REMARC and OCLC. It is anticipated that by July 1988, when the database is loaded into the selected system, there will be about 500,000 monograph titles and 10,000 serial titles in the database. The remaining titles will be loaded by late 1990.

The libraries generate about 200,000 ciculation transactions and 6000 reserve transactions per year.

The Acquisitions Department adds 40,000 items per year with an annual materials expediture of $1,400,000. Serials Records receives about 13,000 subscriptions and checks-in 100,000 items per year. F.W. Faxon is presently the major serials vendor used for U.S. subscriptions. Major approval vendors are Ballen and Harrassowitz.

Acquisition of material is accomplished through a locally written system operating on the University's academic computer.

Cataloging of all material is done through OCLC of Dublin, Ohio, using all of the major MARC formats. OCLC is also used for interlibrary loan. The Libraries are a member of a state-wide network, The _____ Cooperative Library Services Authority.

Adjacent to the campus are two other academic insitutions, with the State University being several miles south of the University. While the initial implementation of an automated system will be limited to this University, the system may be expanded in the future to include one or several other institutions in a network environment.

A Medium Size Special Library (Medical)

The _____ Health Center is one of 16 divisions of the ___
_____ Health Corporation. Located in _____
_____ , it is composed a Children's Hospital, a Neuropsychiatric Hospital, a
General Medical Center, a Professional Office Building and Education Center
and several other units under development.

The Health Center is an antiquated 155 bed in-patient facility. Plans progess
for the completion of a replacement facility that will include expanded child
care services, chemical dependency services, ambulatory care, ambulatory surgery,
and materials management.

The _____ Memorial Library services the information and
library needs of the entire Health Corporation, including its teaching facilities.
There are 2591 employees, 400 attending medical staff, 3 residency training
programs (internal medicine, surgery, and obstetrics and gynecology) for 77
residents and interns. In addition, the hospital has agreements with numerous
schools and colleges .

A Small Size Special Library (Federal)

The NPIC Library serves as a special library for the National Photographic
Interpretation Center and its tenant organization, and it provides standard
reference, loan, current awareness and publication procurement services. Its
collection consists of a mix of books, periodicals, pamphlets, microforms,
newspapers, video cassettes, internally generated classified documents, classified
documents from other souces, and a variety of more sensitive documents requiring
special security controls for each copy. A majority of materials in the collection
is classified. The Appendix indicates the current size of the collection and the
number of items accessioned annually for each type of publication in the
collection.

The purpose of issuing this Request for Proposal (RFP) is to obtain one
automated system that replaces the functions now being performed by a mixture
of manual and automated procedures and that meets the mandatory requirements
as detailed below. This single automated system, generally referred to as an
Integrated Library System (ILS), must be composed of proven, off-the-shelf
software modules and commerically-available hardware. The successful vendor

must be responsible for all facets of the ILS, including but not limited to, hardware, software, data conversion, system installation and user training. Proposals will be evaluated primarily on their technical merits. The cost of the proposed system will be important, but is not the determining factor in the selection of the successful vendor.

The NPIC library is located on the sixth floor of Building 213. It does not have any branches or requirements for terminals in remote locations. The overall space in the library is 5720 square feet. The library has not identified specific space for hardware installation at this time. The library floor plan will be revised contingent on the equipment configuration proposed by the vendor. The library has critical space limitations. therefore the amount of space required will be an important factor in the evaluation of the competing proposals. Proposals must provide explicit information on the size, space, power and air requirements for the hardware. Vendors will be able to inspect the library site and to meet on-site for discussions with library personnel. However, because the work done in the area is classified, vendor's time on-site will be limited. Most of the contract work must be accomplished at the vendor's location.

Special security considerations arise from the nature of the library collection which consists predominatly of classified documents. The library database must be accessed on TEMPEST approved I/O devices. It must be housed on a stand-alone system which is not linked by telecommunications to any device to which uncleared personnel have access. Special procedures must be followed for sensitive documents. These include recording of security control numbers, copy numbers, security classification, and any additional controls or caveats. It also means that someone must record receipt of all copies of these documents which are received in the library, whether the documents are retained or not. When the copies are destroyed, a signed certificate of destruction must be perpared. When such a document is lent, the borrower must sign a receipt indicating that he has possession of the document. Generally speaking, anyone who has access to the library collection will have the clearance to read any of these documents. There are some documents for which this is not true. For these, a library staff person must check the clearances of the library requester before giving access to the document. These documents must be stored separately from the rest of the collection, and some must be housed in safes. The library must be able to lend these materials to library requesters who have the clearances to use them. This means that the library must maintain a record of security clearances in the patron file.

Rules and Conditions

Depending on the governance of the library or local laws and policies, there may exist specific requirements and constraints for the bid process. These should be identified in this section of the RFP. Examples of specific requirements and constraints are given below.

One signed original and fifteen copies of the Proposal and attachments must be sent by certified mail and received no later than 4:00 p.m. EST, Friday, February 27, 198____.

All technical questions dealing with the RFP should be addressed to:_____

_____

All financial question dealing with the RFP should be addressed to:_____

_____

The vendor will render all services under the Agreement in accordance with the applicable provisions of federal, state or local laws, rules or regulations that are in effect at the time the services are rendered.

The vendor and each person signing on behalf of any vendor will represent, warrant and certify, under penalty of perjury, that to the best of its knowledge and belief:

The prices in its proposal have been arrived at independently without collusion, consultation, communication, or agreement, for the purpose of restricting competition, as to any matter relating to such prices with any other vendor or with any competitor; and

Unless otherwise required by law, the prices which have been quoted in the Proposal have not been knowingly disclosed by the vendor prior to the Proposal submission, directly or indirectly, to any other vendor or to any competitor; and

No attempt has been made or will be made by the vendor to induce any other person, partnership or corporation to submit or not to submit a proposal for the purpose of restricting competition; and

The fact that the vendor (1) has published price lists, rates, or tariffs covering items being procured, (2) has informed prospective customers of proposed or pending publication of new or revised price lists for such items, or (3) has sold the same items to other customers at the same prices being bid, does not consititute, without more, a disclosure within the meaning of the above.

The vendor will warrant that the prices, terms, warranties and benefits stated in its Proposal are comparable to, or better than, those offered to the bidder's current clients.

The vendor must agree that all reports, information or data furnished to, prepared, assembled or used by the vendor under the Agreement will be held confidential and protected from disclosure.

Overview of RFP

This section of the RFP is designed to give perspective to the vendors, regarding the intent of the library automation procurement process. It highlights the library's automation goals. A detailed example is given below.

It is the ultimate goal of the library to have a fully integrated automation system which contains modules to accomplish all library functions. It is not feasible within current financial and technological constraints for this RFP to define a specific system design, nor does the library expect any one vendor, in response to this RFP, to propose such a system. Rather, it is the intent to define and acquire a bibliographic database-oriented circulation system and hardware which will have the flexibility and expandability to accomodate the desired fully integrated system.

The library wishes to purchase an integrated library system to be operated on dedicated hardware to be located within the library. A turnkey system is perferred. The modules required are described in order of priority.

The goal of this automation project is to eliminate excessive labor costs resulting from duplicate keying of data, and the inadequacies, inefficiencies and delays experienced in searching for information in miscellaneous sources. Our objectives are as follows:

1. To establish a single integrated library system resident on a single hardware configuration into which all bibliographic data concerning the library collection can be entered.

2. To build all subsequent stages of library processing on the initial data entry.

3. To consult one online public access catalog (OPAC) for bibliographic and subject retrieval of library materials regardless of classification.

4. To track any publication from the point of its initial order through receipt and processing to its permanent location within the collection.

Schedule of Activities

To ensure a fair bid process, a schedule that outlines the selection process should be included in the RFP. The schedule should have the following elements.

o   *Distribution of RFP*

o   *Bidder's Conference*

o   *Deadline for receipt of vendor proposals*

o   *Opening of bids*

o   *Proposal evaluation*

o   *Contract negotiation*

Some libraries may choose not to have a bidder's conference and instead establish deadlines for receiving written requests from vendors for clarification of library automation requirements. In this event, in order to conduct a fair bid process, the library should distribute individual vendor questions and library responses (without identification of specific vendors) to all vendors bidding on the library automation project.

Arrangement of Proposal

In order to facilitate the evaluation process and to ensure continuity of content, the library should specify requirements regarding the organization and format of the vendor proposals.

The Proposal must be arranged in two volumes, with an optional third volume. The first volume shall be the vendor's response to the contract conditions and detailed specifications as detailed in the RFP. The second volume shall be the vendors's financial proposal. If the vendor wishes to include brochures, equipment photos, or other reference materials in the proposal, these materials shall be in the optional third volume. Technical literature, including photographs, pertaining to hardware, software, and other elements of vendor support may be included in this optional volume of the vendor's proposal. Emphasis in the proposal should be placed on completeness and clarity of content.

Each volume should be in a loose-leaf binder with index tabs dividing the sections. Proposals should be prepared on standard 8&1/2 x 11 inch paper (8&1/2 x 14 is permissible for charts, spread sheets, etc.) and placed in loose leaf binders with tabs separating the major sections.

Each vendor may indicate alternate solutions to functions specified in the RFP, and should also indicate the status of those alternatives.

Vendors must respond to each and every functional, technical, and performance requirement contained in the RFP, with a statement of how such requirements will be met. All vendors' responses must be in the same order in which the points appear in this RFP, and must use the same numbering scheme used in this RFP. The vendor's Proposal must be capable of being understood without reference to other documents. Vendors should repeat whatever portions of the text of any supporting documents in their Proposal that are necessary to aid in comprehending the Proposal.

Standardized Description of Development Status

In order to obtain proposals that can be compared readily and to avoid ambiguity of language used in the vendors' proposals, the library should define certain terminology and require the vendors to adhere to these definitions in responding to the RFP.

Vendors are required to respond to all requirements and specifications set forth in this RFP by indicating their current availability using the statuses described in this section.

"Operational"--in production at all user sites (indicate number of sites). If the function is available always at all user sites and some users choose not to use the function, consider the function operational.

"Optionally Available"--conditionally available to all users and in production at some user sites. Indicate equipment, software, costs, and other conditions of availability, the number of user sites using the option, and the names, addresses, and telephone contacts at three (3) sites.

"In Pilot Operation"--in test and evaluation at user sites. Indicate the number of sites, beginning and expected end dates for pilot operation, expected operational date, and names, addresses, and telephone contacts at three (3) pilot sites.

"In Testing"--in-house test and evaluation (capable of being demonstrated). Indicate the expected dates for pilot operation (if applicable) and full operation.

"In Development"--in detailed definition, design, programming, etc. Describe development status, documentation available, and expected operational date.

"In Planning"--in general requirements definition or early planning. Describe available documentation.

"Not Planned"--not expected to be a future function.

Vendors are strongly encouraged to use the terms defined above. Undefined terms relating to development status using the present tense in the proposal will be assumed to mean that the development status is "in planning". General terms where the status is difficult to determine will be assumed to mean "not planned".

THE INFORMATIONAL SECTION

Cover Letter

A cover letter should be required by all vendors submitting bids. The RFP should identify the contents of the cover letter and require that it be signed by an officer of the firm authorized to make the Proposal binding. This letter also can be used by the vendors to describe their qualifications and experience.

The letter of introduction shall be approximately three pages in length; shall include the name and address of the firm submitting the proposal and the name, address and telephone number of the person(s) to contact who shall be authorized to represent the firm; and shall be signed by an officer of the firm authorized to bind the firm to all commitments made in the Proposal.

The vendor will submit a statement describing its organizational structure, the nature and scope of its business operations, its size, number of personnel, number of years in business, and the names of its owners, director, and/or officers. The vendor must identify all key technical personnel it proposes to use in carrying out the terms of the Agreement and will provide information regarding the experience and qualifications of such personnel for performing the requirements of the Agreement. If any of the proposed personnel are independent contractors, then the bidder must so specify and identify the business entity which employs such independent contractor.

The RFP also should instruct the vendors to submit a financial statement indicating the firm's stability within the marketplace.

The vendor also will supply an audited financial statement for the past five (5) years of its operations, or for as many years as it has been in operation if less than five; a Dun & Bradstreet report, if available; the name of the officer, for credit reference purposes, of the financial institution with which it conducts the greatest percentage of its corporate financial services; and any other information that is relevant to its financial stability and solvency.

Table of Contents

The function of the table of contents is to define all material included in the proposal and identify it by sequential page number and by section reference. This should be specified in the RFP. (See Figure 3.1)

Management Summary

The primary purpose of the management summary is to familiarize uninitiated and non-technical readers who have an interest in the library's automation program, such as administrators and boards of trustees, with the general aspects of the proposed system. It can be requested in the RFP using the following language.

The management summary should contain a brief statement of the salient features of the proposed system and a review of the distinctive merits of the proposed system. The summary should be readily understandable by non-technical personnel at the management level and should be no more than three double-spaced pages in length.

References

The RFP should state the following reference requirements.

Each vendor is required to submit a list of names of contact persons, addresses, and telephone numbers of all users of the systems similar to the one proposed for the library. Each vendor shall report what equipment present customers are using for disk storage, the amount of disk storage being used, the amount of main memory, the total annual circulation, the number of titles, copies, and borrowers in the online files, and the number of terminals being used. A survey of references will be made to determine, among other things, the service availability for vendor equipment and software currently installed at customer locations. In taking the survey, if it is revealed that the average annual availability of the system is less than what is required by the library (98%), the proposal may be eliminated from futher consideration.

50

Evaluation Process

It is standard procedure to describe in the RFP the criteria to be used in evaluating the vendor proposals. This is done in order to give the vendors an opportunity to submit the most complete and competitive bids possible. An example of this section of the RFP follows.

The library, with the assistance of a consultant, will review and evaluate all proposals received. To receive proper consideration, the proposals should meet the requirements of the RFP and should be presented in the prescribed specified format. The evaluation will credit only those capabilities and advantages which are clearly stated in the vendor's written proposal. The evaluation methodology to be used will be the one most advantageous to the library. Proposals meeting the requirements of this RFP will be evaluated principally in the following areas (in priority order): compliance with system specifications; response times; system reliability (both hardware and software); maintenance support; costs; flexibility; training/documentation; past performance on installing automated library systems and delivery schedule; capability for system expansion and upgrading; and financial credibility of the vendor.

Rejection of Proposals

This section of the RFP gives the library an opportunity to exercise flexibility in the procurement process. It also reminds the vendor that this is a negotiated bid process and does not require that the library award a contract to the lowest bidder.

The library reserves the right to reject any and all proposals received in response to this RFP. Nonacceptance of any proposal will not imply any criticism of the proposal or convey any indication that the proposal or proposed system was deficient. Nonacceptance of any proposal will mean that another proposal was deemed to be more advantageous to the library or that no proposal was deemed acceptable. The library reserves the right to accept other than the lowest price proposal and to negotiate with any vendor when the best interests of the library are served by so doing. All materials submitted in response to this RFP become the property of the library.

Withdrawal of Proposals

The library will expend many resources in evaluating each vendor proposal received. These resources would be wasted if any of the vendors withdrew their proposal during or after the evaluation. Therefore, it behooves the library to describe in the RFP the specific procedures and penalties for early withdrawal. Examples of the procedures and penalties for withdrawal of proposals are described below.

Any vendor may withdraw its proposal, either personally or by written or telegraphic request, at any time prior to (date), provided that written confirmation of any telegraphic withdrawal over the signature of the vendor is placed in the mail and postmarked prior to (same time and date as above). No proposal may be withdrawn or modified after this date, unless and until the award of the contract is delayed for a period exceeding one hundred twenty (120) days. Negligence on the part of the vendor in preparing its proposal confers no right of withdrawal or modification of the proposal after such proposal has been opened. Violation of these procedures may cause the vendor to forfeit its proposal guarantee. (See Proposal Guarantee below).

Note that the dates included in this section should be the same as the date for opening the bids.

Addendum and Supplement to the RFP

As mentioned earlier, there are two methods by which vendors might obtain additional information to supplement the library's RFP. The library decides which method will be employed. If the library chooses, for example, to conduct a vendor's conference, the language used in the RFP should so state.

A vendor's conference will be held at _____ on _ _____. Each section of this RFP will be reviewed. Vendors are urged to identify specific sections and paragraphs requiring clarification prior to the discussion to permit an orderly review. These should be mailed to_____ _____*to ensure that they are placed on the agenda.*

On the other hand the library may choose, in lieu of a vendor's conference, to receive written requests for clarification from the vendors. The wording in the RFP for this purpose may be as follows.

The library has decided to waive a vendor's conference in lieu of the RFP clarification procedure specified below.

Questions and requests for clarification concerning this RFP must be submitted in writing no later than (time and date). The words "Automated System Inquiry" should apppear on the envelope. Inquries must state the page and applicable RFP section or paragraph number(s) to which the question(s) pertain.

All clarification or addenda to the RFP shall be distributed in writing to all participating vendors. The source of an inquiry occasioning a clarification shall not be given. This RFP and all subsequent modifications thereto are hereby designated as the sole reference and authority for the preparation of proposals, and take precedence over any and all information related to the acquisition obtained from any source either by verbal or written communication. Clarification and/or addenda will be distributed no later than_____

THE SPECIAL REQUIREMENTS SECTION

Proposal Guarantee

As a guarantee that the vendors will abide by the procedures for withdrawal of proposals, and that the selected vendor will execute the terms of the contract, each Proposal shall be accompanied by a guarantee which shall be equal to at least ten per cent (10%) of the base Proposal and at the option of the vendor may be:

a) A certified check, or

b) A bank cashier's check, or

c) a bid bond from a SURETY COMPANY LICENSED IN THE STATE OF_____.

The successful vendor's proposal gurantee will be returned after a contract has been signed. The library reserves the right to hold the Proposal Guarantees of all vendors until it has entered into contract, or for a period of one hundred twenty (120) days from the date of the bid openning, whichever is the shorter time.

In some instances the library may wish to retain the successful vendor Proposal Guarantee as the Performance Bond until after the full terms of the contract have been met by the vendor. An alternative method for protecting the interest of the library is discussed under the section PAYMENT SCHEDULE below.

Vendor's Cost to Develop Proposal

Cost to develop the vendors' proposals is considered as their overhead cost and should not be chargeable to the library.

Costs for developing proposals in response to this RFP are entirely the obligation of the vendor and shall not be charged to the library in any manner.

Proposal Validity Period

As a complement to the Proposal Guarantee clause in the RFP, the following language should also be included in the RFP.

Submission of a proposal will signify the vendor's agreement that the proposal is valid for one hundred twenty (120) days from the date of the bid opening.

Payment Schedule

If negotiated properly, the payment schedule can be used in lieu of a performance bond in order to protect the interest of the library. The strategy for negotiating the payment schedule is discussed in Chapter 5, Negotiating the Contract. It is appropriate, however, to include in the RFP a payment schedule for the vendors. An example is given below.

All payments to the vendor shall be remitted by mail. Drafts shall not be honored nor goods accepted on a sight draft basis. Furthermore, the provisions or monies due under this contract shall be assignable. Payments will be made as follows (1) at delivery____%; (2) at installation completion____%; and (3) upon completion of all acceptance tests____%,____%,____% and ____%___ respectively.

News Releases

Because of the high competition within the library automation marketplace, vendors naturally will want to capitalize on publicity gained from winning a library's automation contract. Particularly if the library is a large or prestigious library, the successful vendor will want to make public the nature of the automation contract award. It is in the best interest of the library always to retain control of any publicity stemming from the automation program. The RFP should make this clear to all vendors submitting bids.

News releases pertaining to an award resulting from proposals made in response to this RFP will not be made by any vendor without prior written approval from the library administration. Any information which may have been released, whether verbally or in writing, prior to the issuance of the contract award for the the system selected or pertaining to the RFP shall be disregarded and not considered in the evaluation of any proposal.

Training Program

The requirements for staff training must be identified clearly in the RFP for two important reasons: 1) to ensure that the selected vendor has the resources and knows the methodology to train staff adequately on the new system; 2) to prevent attributing any system failure to an inadequately trained staff. The library can protect itself in these regards by placing the following statements in the RFP.

The proposed system must not require a high level of data processing expertise at the CPU site or in any of the branch sites that use the system. Each vendor must include in the proposal a description of the training program that is proposed. This description must include a list of trainers, their qualifications, and the proposed training methods and schedules. The selected vendor must provide training, at no additional cost, for the following groups.

a. Supervisory and administrative staff: overall system work flow, operations, and troubleshooting. The minimum number of supervisory and administrative persons to be trained will be _____.

b. Library public service staff: daily operations and procedures for relevant system functions. The vendor must provide on-site instruction for sufficient time to allow all appropriate public service staff to master the operations of the system.

c. Conversion teams: conversion techniques in labeling and developing borrower and item files. The minimum of staff persons to be trained will be _____.

The selected vendor must be prepared to certify in writing that the staff is adequately trained to operate and maintain the system prior to the performance of any acceptance testing.

Documentation

In addition to specifying the types of documentation required by the library, the RFP should request that each vendor submit, as part of their proposal, samples of the documentation listed below. It also will be helpful to discover through this section, if vendors are able to deliver their user documentation in an electronic format, so that the library has the flexibility of editing and formatting it for their specific needs.

The selected vendor must provide _____ printed user manuals for terminal operators, and _____ printed manuals for the CPU site operators that describe such activities as recovery, file back-up, tape loading, disk mounting, and report production.

The vendor must provide complete system documentation, including file description, system flows, and equipment usage manuals. These manuals must be detailed enough to allow authorized staff to use the system for special reports or other functions.

All revisions and upgrades to manuals provided must be supplied by the vendor at no additional cost to the library.

It is desired that, in addition to the printed manuals, online equivalent texts be provided if available.

Each vendor is required to submit samples of its user manuals and its system operator manuals.

THE SYSTEM SPECIFICATION SECTION (Functional and Technical Specifications)

In the introduction to the RFP section on system specifications there should be an attempt to standardize the language that will be used to convey the priorities of the library's automated system. This introduction should provide some background information concerning the library and its environment and restate the library's goals concerning the implementation of an automated system, including expectations for future growth. The following example shows how the system specification may be introduced in the RFP.

Language Conventions

In this section of this RFP, an attempt is made to standardize the language used to indicate the relative importance of a specification. The word "must" and the phrase "it is required that" are invariably used in connection with a mandatory specification; the word "should" is invariably used in connection with a specification that has a very high priority, but is not mandatory; the phrase "it is desirable" is invariably used in connection with a specification that has a high priority, but is not mandatory. These specification describe functions or features that will be used by the library.

In the text of this document, "online, computer-based integrated library system" shall be synonymous with "system" and not with "library system".

The system must operate in a real time, conversational mode, and, to the highest degree possible, be data independent, to allow for changes in applications without rewriting programs.

Statistical Information

In addition to the background information provided earlier, this section of the RFP should refer vendors to appendices within the RFP which include statistical and other detailed information concerning the library and the implementation plan.

Detailed statistical information about the library is given in Appendix _____. Information about the number and location of terminals is given in Appendix ___ _. Information about the locations and relative distances between branch libraries is given in Appendix _____.

Goals and Objectives

The library's automation program goals and objectives should be stated in detail in this section of the RFP.

The library requires a reliable and flexible, computer-based integrated library system with online data files and a proven ability to operate more efficiently and effectively than the system now being used. The system must be operable by trained library staff and must not require a high level of data processing expertise on the part of the staff. The system must enable the library to achieve the following objectives (in order of priority).

1) a reduction in the amount of time involved in completing circulation transactions and an increase in the efficiency and accuracy with which those transactions are carried out;

2) the ability to determine, quickly and accurately, what titles are in the collection, how many copies are owned, location of copies, current status of copies, and due date if charged out;

3) the ability to determine, quickly and accurately, the current status of a borrower, including the borrower's address and telephone number; and

4) an increase in the efficiency with which materials may be transferred from one branch location to another.

Future Growth

For any automated library system to be cost effective, it is essential to be able to support the future work load requirements of the library for a minimum of five years. This requirement should be clearly stated in the RFP.

The proposed system must have the equipment and software capacity to accommodate the complete aggregate collection of the library, including growth in collection size and borrower population through 1991, and the transaction load represented by all current and projected service locations, without degradation to the system in any way. This includes transaction response time, up-time rate, and functionality. The system must be easily expandable to accommodate subsystems such as acquisitions, administration, on-line catalog, and serials.

Depending on the future work load requirements for the system, the library may allow an exception to some of the future equipment requirements. This exception is made usually for the number of disk packs and controllers.

System Specifications

There will be three major categories of system specifications included in the RFP: 1)Functional; 2) Technical; and 3)Performance. Methods for writing each are reviewed below along with examples for each of the three.

Functional Specifications

Using the language conventions described above, that indicate the mandatory and desired requirements each functional specification is written to convey to the vendor the importance or priority of the specific requirement. Writing the specifications is a deductive process whereby each major activity is analyzed in terms of its smallest operational component. The functional specification describes what it is the system is expected to do. The Charge Function is an example of functional specifications that would be included in this section of the RFP.

Charge Function

Definition: a procedure by which a library lends an item or items from its collection (interlibrary loan inclusive) to an eligible borrower for a specified length of time.

a) The system must be able to charge out items to special borrowers and to record the status of items charged out to the bindery, lost or missing.

b) The system must choose automatically the appropriate loan period based on the category of borrower and the type and format of item.

c) If an item presented for charge by a borrower was never discharged, the system must automatically discharge it, flag the item record, and continue the charge transaction. The system must have the capability to produce, on demand, a report which lists these items.

The charge function and the breakdown of its functional specification might then be followed by the renewal function, the discharge function, the overdue/fine function, notice function and other applicable functions.

The procedure for generating the circulation functional specifications would be used for other subsystems, such as acquisition, serials, and cataloging. (See Appendix B for a complete list of functional specifications for each of these sub-systems).

Technical Specifications

Writing the technical specifications makes use of the same language conventions that were used to write the functional specification (i.e., must, should, it is desired that). The purpose is to convey to the vendor the importance or priority of a particular technical specification. Arriving at technical specifications also is an analytical process that examines each functional specification in order to determine how the functional specification will be met. Here the library should exercise caution not to overspecify the requirement. Too much emphasis on telling the vendor(s) how a particular technical specification should be carried out may reduce the flexibility with which the vendor responds to the requirement. It also may lead to the situation where the library has to assume the responsibility for a feature within the system that is inappropriate or does not work.

The objective in writing technical specifications is to solicit information from the vendor(s) that can be used by the library to evaluate whether the vendor's proposed system can meet the automation goals and objectives of the library. An example of a technical specification which has correspondence to the charge function might be as follows.

The system must be supported by a CPU or CPUs that will insure a response rate of two (2) seconds or less for all charge transactions for all 50 terminals at peak loads. The vendors, in addition, must specify the following information:

    o model and memory capacity of CPU,

    o access and cycle time of CPU,

    o total number of configurations of this size
      installed to date (identify exact sites), and

    o maximum number of terminals the CPU will support, as configured,
      without loss of response time.

Note that by requesting specific information concerning the hardware, in the context of this technical specification, the library will be able to judge independently the ability of the proposed system to perform the specification. An example of a complete list of technical specifications appear in Appendix C.

Performance Specifications

The primary purpose of the performance specification is to identify constraints and desirable methods by which a particular functional or technical requirement will be met by the automated system. Again, it is important that the performance specification not be overly prescriptive. A performance specification that may accompany the above technical specification is follows.

The vendor must guarantee a two (2) second response time without specifying the need for additional memory, however, background/ foreground processing are acceptable.

Miscellaneous Specifications

There are a variety of other types of system specifications that, while labeled miscellaneous, are still very important for inclusion in the RFP.

File Design Specifications

The file structure must be integrated with a suitable data base management system.

The system must accept and differentiate among all existing MARC bibliographic formats and accommodate all fields of the MARC II formats.

The system must allow all MARC fields to be added, deleted or changed and must have full MARC record imput and output capability.

Other aspects of file design to be covered under the file specifications include: file access, authority control, cataloging maintenance, and borrower file. For a complete list of these specifications, see Appendix D.

Data Security and Recovery

The system must provide security to prevent accidental or unauthorized modification of records.

The system must provide two pyramid structures of authorization which are independent of each other. The terminal identification pyramid is to have two levels:

a. the highest level must have access to all apects of the system, both equipment and software, including the ability to alter the authorization of these terminals;

b. the second level must permit circulation function overrides and alteration of patron, bibliographic and item records.

The operator identification pyramid is to have four levels:

a. the highest level must permit access to all levels of the applications software, including the ability to alter the authorization level of all other operator identification codes;

b. the second level must permit alteration of patron, bibliograhic, and item records and overrides of circulation functions;

c. the third level must permit overrides of circulation functions;

d. the fourth level must permit "read-only" access to bibliographic and item records.

Provisions for Downtime

It is required that the proposed system include some provision for continuing at least charge and discharge transactions when the system is down. Such provision must not require any manual logging of transactions for keying at a later time and must not involve the use of cassette devices for logging transaction data. It such provision involves collection of transaction data by means of a solid state portable terminal, the system must provide for quick and efficient input of this data once the system is up. Each vendor must provide detailed description of these procedures, including time to input a given number of transactions.

Equipment List and System Diagram

In order to facilitate comparing the proposals and to cross check the individual components offered by the vendors as part of the total system, the RFP should request that each vendor submit an itemized list of equipment and diagrams using forms designed by the library and exhibited in the RFP. Figure 3.2 illustrates a form that can be adapted for this purpose. An example of the language that can be used in this section of the RFP is given here.

Using the enclosed forms, each vendor must include an itemized list of all equipment proposed. Do not include price information on the equipment list. All information requested for each component and all equipment specifications requested in this RFP should be included with the equipment list.

Item	Quantity	Model/Manufacturer	Functional Description

Table 3.2

Equipment List Form

THE FINANCIAL SECTION

Pricing Information

For the purpose of easy comparison between proposals, price reporting within the various vendor proposals should be done in as a standard method as possible. (Figure 3.3 provides an example of a Price Quotation Form.) This form then can be compared to the Equipment List Form (Figure 3.2) for any discrepencies.

Each vendor must provide pricing information for the proposed system on a Price Quotation Form. All equipment proposed must appear on the Price Quotation Form. The equipment listed on the Equipment List Form of the proposal and the equipment listed on the Price Quotation Form should be identical except for price information.

QUANTITY	ITEM DESCRIPTION	MANUFACTURER & MODEL NO	UNIT COST	TOTAL COST	MONTHLY MAINTENANCE

Figure 3.3

Price Quotation Form

Courtesy Neal-Schuman Publishers Inc.

Financial Alternatives

In some instances the library may have the flexibility to choose from several alternative methods to finance the purchase of the automated system, particularly if one method may be in the best interest of the library. The vendors, through the RFP, should be given an opportunity to describe such alternatives.

In addition to providing financial information for outright purchase and ongoing maintenance, each vendor must provide financial information for the following alternative(s), or state that the alternative(s) is not available:

   a. five (5) year installment purchase;
   b. five (5) year lease with purchase options;
   c. five (5) year lease.

The financial information for each alternative proposed must be supplied on a separate Price Quotation Form. Vendors may, at their option, propose other financial alternatives.

Additional Price Information

There are several additional types of inquiries that should be presented to the vendors concerning costs.

What is the maximum percentage the maintenance rate will be increased in any fiscal year?

Specify a price for barcode lables that is quaranteed for twelve (12) months following acceptance of the proposal and the awarding of the contract.

Specify the cost to the library of the interfaces among any proposed systems. If there is no separate identifiable cost, so indicate.

Specify any costs chargeable to the library for the initial loading of the bibliographic data.

Note: It is assumed that all costs specified as part of this section are included in the total purchase price of the proposed system shown on the Price Quotation

Form.

Specify the costs of the initial stock of supplies.

Specify the cost of any additional equipment, telecommunications, terminals, supplies, etc. for each subsystem.

For a complete list of sample miscellaneous system specifications see Appendix D.

Prices and Price Protection

"Most favored nation" is the legal concept that ensures that the library will benefit from the prices that the current market will bear. The language used to describe this concept in the RFP, together with language that uncovers any hidden costs is described below.

Each vendor must provide complete price schedules for all equipment and services proposed. Any element of recurring or non-recurring cost which must be borne by the library must be identified. This includes, but is not limited to: equipment maintenance, system engineering, manuals and documentation, education/training, bibliographic conversion, demonstration, consultation, shipping charges, installation costs (excluding site preparation), testing, taxes, and manufacturer supplied programs. Rental rates and license fees, proposed, if any, shall be the maximum permitted during the term of the contract(s) executed by the library as a result of this acquisition. Vendors may propose either firm prices (lease, purchase, and maintenance), valid for the term of the contract(s), or propose prices with periodic incremental increases which will be evaluated financially at their maximum allowable value. Maintenance rate increases shall be permitted only upon written notice to the library at the termination of its fiscal year. Each vendor must specify in the proposal an upper limit percentage beyond which maintenance rates will not increase in any calendar year.

If the vendor receives a lower OEM (Original Equipment Manufacturer) price of maintenance rate for any equipment identified in the vendor's proposal during the negotiation and contract period, the library shall have the benefit of such lower price, and the vendor shall notify the library accordingly and make the necessary reductions.

Presentation of Prices and Taxes

All designations and prices shall be fully and clearly set forth and shall include all applicable federal and state taxes, including sales taxes. Those applicable taxes shall be itemized fully in the proposal and shall be also included in determining the sum total of the proposal amount. The library shall consider sales taxes to be included in any proposal which shows only a total amount proposed without presenting itemized details of the individual cost components of the proposal.

In the event that the library is a tax-free institution the RFP in this section should so state, and should present the library's tax-exempt identification number.

THE CONTRACT SECTION

Contractual Specifications

It is in the interest of the library to determine, as best it can, through the RFP, which vendors have the highest willingness to negotiate a contract if selected as the most competitive vendor. Contract negotiation can be a lengthy and difficult process and requires a fair amount of give and take on the part of both the library and the vendor. A method for determining the ability of the vendor to negotiate is described below and should be included in the RFP.

General Contractual Requirements

This section of the RFP identifies required terms and conditions that must be included in the contract(s) and executed as a result of this acquisition. Each of the following terms and conditions must be answered by each vendor submitting a proposal. The terms and conditions have been designated as either: 1) Mandatory, Verbatim (MV), which means that to be considered responsive, the vendor must agree to execute a contract(s) that includes the terms or conditions exactly as written; 2) Mandatory, Content (MC) which means that to be considered responsive, the vendor must agree to execute a contract(s) that includes language addressing the general intent of the provision as written.

(MV) No advance payment shall be made for goods or services furnished by contractor pursuant to this contract.

(MC) Contractor, its agents, employees or subcontractors shall conform in all respects with physical, fire or other published security regulations while on the library's premises.

For a complete list of typical Mandatory, Verbatim and Mandatory, Content terms and conditions of an automated library system contract see Appendix E.

Chapter Four

FINAL SELECTION AND IMPLEMENTATION

Evaluation of Vendor Proposals
System Evaluation and Final Acceptance

EVALUATION OF VENDOR PROPOSALS

Chapter Two discussed the preliminary review techniques used to select those vendors, which by virtue of their responsiveness to the library's RFP, would be further evaluated. This evaluation and selection process should be formal and systematic and as quantitative as possible.

Having narrowed the list of candidate systems, there remains a set of alternatives, each of which generally meets the mandatory requirements of the automated library system. Additional analysis is necessary to determine the degree to which these mandatory requirements are met by each vendor, and the extent to which desirable requirements are available for each of the alternatives.

The formal selection process makes use of the mandatory specifications found in the RFP by listing them in a vendor requirement matrix. Figure 4.1 is an example. As specified in the library's RFP, an automated system is required to perform all the major functions associated with the circulation of materials at an acceptable level. Priority is assigned to each category of requirments, and each vendor is assessed in terms of the degree to which it meets the mandatory requirement, from nonresponsive (1) to exceeding the specification (4).

The next step in the formal selection process considers cost factors to determine which vendor will be invited to negotiate a contract. Costs should be categorized as current and future. The current costs are those specified in the financial sections of the vendor proposals. Future costs are those which are charged to each desired requirement not met by the vendor, the logic being that the vendor's inability to supply the requirement is a potential additional expense to be incurred by the library. This will provide a "total cost" for each remaining vendor package.

What remains, before final selection can be made, is the calculation of a cost-effective ratio for each vendor. This is achieved by dividing the total system's cost for each by the score in the mandatory requirements category. See Figure 4.2 for an example, where cost/performance ratios are obtained by dividing the cost of the system by the vendor's weighted performance score (x1000) from Figure 4.1.

SYSTEM EVALUATION AND FINAL ACCEPTANCE

Part of implementing the automated library system requires evaluating it for performance. Evaluation occurs in phases, each phase being tied to a payment schedule as noted in the purchase contract. Upon successful completion of a series of evaluation tests, the library accepts the automated system. These tests are described below.

System Reliability Test: Once the automated library system is delivered and is in place, the vendor should certify that it is operational and ready for use. This certification can be based on a demonstration that the library's database can be loaded by the automated library system.

MANDATORY FUNCTIONAL SPECIFICATIONS

SPECIFICATIONS	PRIORITY	OPTION 1		OPTION 2		OPTION 3	
	RATING	WT.	SCORE	WT.	SCORE	WT.	SCORE
Charge-out	3	3	9	2	6	3	9
Renewals	2	3	6	3	6	2	4
Discharges	3	2	6	3	9	3	9
Overdue fine	3	3	9	2	6	3	9
Notice funct.	3	3	9	2	6	3	9
Purge funct.	1	2	2	3	3	3	3
Branch tfr.	2	3	6	2	4	3	6
OCLC interface	3	3	9	2	6	3	9
Hold function	2	3	6	2	4	3	6
Back-up	3	2	6	1	3	4	12
ILL (outside)	1	2	2	2	2	2	2
Report funct.	2	4	8	2	4	4	8
Invt. funct.	3	3	9	2	6	3	9
Inquiry funct.	3	2	6	2	6	4	12
Message funct.	1	3	3	2	2	3	3
Misc.	1	4	4	3	3	3	3
TOTAL SCORE			100		76		113
COST/PERFORMANCE			2.6		3.9		2.3

PRIORITY RATING   WEIGHT   SCORE = P.R. x W

High -> Low = 3 -> 1   4 = exceeds specification
                         3 = adequate
                         2 = minimally adequate
                         1 = nonresponsive

Figure 4.1

Vendor Requirement Matrix

Courtesy Neal-Schuman Publishers Inc.

	OPTION 1	OPTION 2	OPTION 3	
MANDATORY FUNCTIONAL SPECS	100	76	113	SCORE
	$260,936	$300,546	$246,700	COST
	2.6	3.9	2.3	C/P
MANDATORY TECHNICAL SPECS	93	88	92	SCORE
	$260,936	$300,546	$246,700	COST
	2.8	3.4	2.8	C/P
DESIRABLE SPECS	6	6	9	SCORE
	$289,756	$300,546	$246,700	COST
	48.2	50.0	29.0	C/P

* available at additional cost

Figure 4.2

Cost/Performance Ratios

Courtesy Neal-Schuman Publishers Inc.

The system reliabilty test requires that the installed system operate at a prespecified level of effectiveness for prespecified periods of time. (Level of effectiveness is measured by the ability of the system to perform required tasks for a period of time without failure.) A standard for this test is that the system operate at a 98 % level of effectiveness for sixty consecutive work days. The formula for determining system reliability is:

Level of Effectiveness = Total no. of operating hours of the system

Total no. operating hours the system is needed (specified by lib.)

If the average "downtime" is more than was specified in the test, the system has not met its level of effectiveness, and the system reliability test begins again. At the time of contract negotiation, the number of days which the vendor has to meet the prespecified level of effectiveness should have been established.

The importance of the system reliability test should not be underestimated by the library. Using the 98 % level of effectiveness for a period of sixty consecutive work days as a standard, this translates into 1.2 days of downtime or an average of 7.2 days per year. (Hegerty, 1981.) For any automated circulation system this would be the maximum affordable time to be unavailable to carry out charge and discharge transactions. Figure 4.3 is an example of a log used to record the results of the system reliability test.

Functional Validity Test: The purpose of this test is to verify that the automated library system performs each function as described in the library's list of specifications. The test has each function performed separately and then evaluated against the specific requirments established for that function. The primary criteria examined are the accuracy with which the function is performed and the ease with which the operator of the system can execute the function.

LOG FOR SYSTEM RELIABILITY TEST

System Reliability Test

Downtime Cases	Downtime Coefficient Factors*

Case 1 - CPU, Disk Subsystem
            and Console   1.00

Case 2 - Terminals. Modems and
            Ports

1-4	remote terminals	.25
5-9	remote terminals	.50
10-14	remote terminals	.75
14+	remote terminals	1.00

Case 3 - Wands, Slave, Printers
            and System Printer   .40

Downtime (in hours) = number of downtime hours x downtime
                      coefficient factor

e.g., 6 terminals down for 3 hours
Total downtime = 3 x .50 or 1.5 downtime hours

720 hours for 30 days = 100% up-time
Minimum up-time in hours is 706 hours for a 98% up-time rate
or no more than 14 downtime hours.

System Reliability Test: Daily Summary Log

DATE: /   /

TIME CASE WENT DOWN: _____ (a.m./p.m.)

DESCRIPTION OF FAILURE/ERRORS/OMISSIONS:

SOLUTION:

TOTAL CASE
DOWNTIME _____

* The coefficient factors are determined by a priority judgement
  and assures fairness in that disconnection time in proportionate
  to the adverse impact the organization would experience in the
  event of specific system failure.

Figure 4.3

Log for System Reliability Test

Courtesy Neal-Schuman Publishers Inc.

The functional validity test is performed after the system reliability test and should be conducted only when the library is fully prepared to simulate the conditions under which the actual function will be performed. Similarly, the data processed during the test should be representative of the data-- if not the actual data-- with which the system will eventually work. Figure 4.4 is an example of a log which can be used during the functional validity test. Note that in addition to testing the actual available functions, the log allows one to record the characteristics and status of the function as described in the library's RFP, the vendor's proposal and the vendor's user manual. This method of reporting and evaluating functions is particularly important for those functions which are currentlynot available on the system, but promised by the vendor as a future deliverable.

Full-load Performance Test: This test is intended to demonstrate the ability of the automated library system to maintain its level of effectiveness, to perform all functions, and to respond quickly under stress. The full-load performance test is designed to evaluate the potential capacity of the system by simulating peak-load conditions. The following is an example of a full-load performance test used to evaluate the capacity of an automated library circulation system.

"For circulation control, full-load shall mean X(x=n number of terminals) terminals operating at circulation performing at a minimum of Y(y=n number of transactions) check-out and check-in transactions per minute, per terminal. At least Z (z=n number of terminals) terminals shall be remotely connected to the computer telephone lines. W (w= n number of terminals) terminals shall be operating as inquiry terminals performing patron, author, call number, and title inquiries and a minimum of V (V=n number of inquiries) inquiries per minute shall be made per terminal. U (U=n number of terminals) terminals to enter title and item information at the rate of T (T=n number of items per hour). At some point during the test, data from a portable terminal shall simultaneously prepare and print overdue notices, patron notices, or management reports. The full-load performance test for the circulation control system will commence when at least fifty percent (50%) of the library's collection has been converted to machine-readable form." (Hegerty, 1981). See Appendix C for examples of technical specifications.

Figure 4.5 is an example of a log which can be used with the full-load performance test described above. The log is used to derive the average response time of the system. It is calculated by dividing the total of all transaction times by the total number of transactions.

REFERENCE

Hegerty, Kevin. *More Joy of Contracts*. Tacoma, WA: Tacoma Public Library, 1981.

REQUIRED	NEGOTIABLE	ITEM #*	SPECIFICATIONS	REF. NO.**	COMPLIANCE	NON-COMPLIANCE	COMMENTS
		1.1	The system must be able to handle cross tabulation of statistics for management reporting.	V.P. V.4.8.2 REQ III.4.2 U.M. X.1.2			

* Refers to the numbered list of specifications usually found in the Request For Proposal.

** Refers to the references found in the vendor proposal, the vendor's response to the Request For Quotation and the User Manual for the proposed system.

Figure 4.4

Log for Functional Validity Test

CIRCULATION (BOOK CHARGE AND DISCHARGE TRANSACTIONS)

Total number of transactions completed in 1 hour per terminal:

1. _____
2. _____
3. _____
4. _____
5. _____
6. _____
7. _____
8. _____
9. _____
10. _____

Total number of transactions: _____

Response time for system: _____
(60/total number of trans-
 actions for all terminals)

INQUIRY

Total number of inquiries completed in one hour per terminal:

11. _____
12. _____
13. _____
14. _____

Total number of inquiries: _____

Response time for system: _____
(60/total number of inquiries
 for all terminals)

Figure 4.5

Log for Full-Load Performance Test

Courtesy Neal-Schuman Publishers Inc.

Chapter Five

WRITING AND NEGOTIATING THE CONTRACT

Drafting the Automation Contract
Negotiating the Contract
On-going Management of the Automated System

DRAFTING THE AUTOMATION CONTRACT

The purchase contract for acquiring an automated library system is a complicated document to write. The nature of automated systems requires that careful attention be given to the drafting of the sales contract in order to protect the interests of the library. Accepting the vendor's standard contract, without making significant changes to it, is rarely recommended because it is intended to protect, almost exclusively, the interests of the vendor. In re-drafting the automation contract, however, the library should be aware of a double-edged sword. A general rule of contract construction is that ambiguities in drafting are resolved against the drafter.

The automation contract should be drafted by the library's legal representative in consultation with the project management staff. The document should incorporate not only product expectations, but also which hardware and software components the vendor has recommended to meet those expectations. The hardware and software components should be described and specified unit by unit to determine if the vendor warrants component compatibility for both basic and peripheral equipment.

The following checklist covers some typical terms and conditions to consider in a library automation acquisition contract. It is abbreviated in content and not meant to be all inclusive, but is intended as a basic guideline to assist in developing lists relative to the librarys' own situations. Appendix E provides a more detailed list of contract terms and conditions, as well as an example of a library automation contract.

I. Is the contract written in terms of the results expected by the library in acquiring an automated library system (e.g., circulation control, catalog maintenance, aquisitions control, materials booking,)?

II. Are hardware and software specified unit by unit?

III. Does the contract incorporate detailed specifications regarding computer system performance, including the following items.

   A. Specific functions the vendor indicates will be done (e.g. providing reserve lists, circulation statistics, patron delinquency lists, online database inquiry).

   B. What the vendor will do regarding the following.
     1. site preparation
     2. date and method of delivery--penalties for delay
     3. installation
     4. compatibility of components
     5. documentation

6. providing personnel
7. staff training
8. testing
9. guarantees of reliability
10. security of database and equipment
11. confidentiality of users (patrons and library)
12. maintenance
13. modifications and upgrading

C. What the library will do regarding the following items
   1. site preparation
   2. providing qualified staff
   3. accepting delivery after testing

IV. Financial Matters
   A. Are lease, purchase, timesharing or service bureau terms clear, accurate, and mutually understood?
   B. What discounts apply?
   C. What tax issues should be discussed?
   D. What are the penalties for partial or non-performance?
   E. What backups are there for downtime?
   F. What are the payment schedules and contingencies for payment?

V. In urance
   A. What coverage is there for damage to, or injury resulting from, equipment or personnel?
   B. What coverage is there for damage to the database?

Special Considerations. With the foregoing as background, it is easy to see that the importance of a well-drafted contract hardly can be overstated. The rules under which the procurement of an automated library system will be governed should be articulated precisely to avoid later conflicts arising from ambiguity and misunderstandings.

During the course of selection and evaluation, the vendor will make a wide range of representations in its proposal as to the capabilities of the automated library system and how these capabilities will fullfill the library's needs. Brochures or specification sheets containing photographs and descriptions of the equipment and its performance characteristics often are included. Additionally, letters may be exchanged detailing the speed and efficiency of a particular function or system activity. Sales personnel also may make verbal representations regarding maintenance, hardware and software support, training and installation.

Almost invariably, however, the library finds a clause in the vendor's standard contract for which there are no understandings or agreements between the parties except as specified in the written contract and that the vendor has no obligations to the library except as expressly set forth in the contract. This so-called "merger" or "integration" clause generally is held to be valid in contract construction.

To help alleviate the effect of the integration clause, the library should make sales documents and the vendor's proposal part of the binding automation contract by including them as attachments. Additionally, it is essential that the vendor's performance obligations regarding both hardware and software be defined precisely and in sufficient technical detail. This can be done by incorporating functional and technical specifications from the library's RFP and making it clear that such specifictions are the criteria by which to measure the vendor's performance. Also, since most procurement contracts disclaim any "implied" warrantees, such as that the automated system is designed for a particular purpose, the library, in drafting its contract should include "express" warrantees that relate to system performance, response time, reliability, etc. It is advisable to avoid terms such as "turnkey", "management information system", etc. when expressing system requirements for purposes of precision and clarity.

The library should be aware, however, that the process of specifying functional characteristics of the automated library system in the contract in connection with the integration clause can limit the legal rights the library might otherwise have under the law. Careful consultation with the library's legal representative in this matter is, therefore, in order.

The automation contract should specify the payment schedules and their relationship to certain milestones such as delivery, installation and acceptance testing. The contract also might provide for liquidated damages in the event specified milestones are not met. The terms for liquidated damages should include a provision which expressly allows the library to recover its implementation and reprocurement costs if the vendor's system proves inadequate and the library is required to seek an alternative system. This provision should provide for the recovery of costs involving data conversion and consultant and attorney fees used in selecting the new system.

With respect to choice of law provision, the library may be bound to the governance of its home state as the client in the transaction. However, if there exists flexibility in choosing between the home state in which the vendor is located and the library's own state, it is wise to research the statutory and case laws of the respective states to determine which governing laws may be most favorable to the library.

Finally, in drafting the automation contract the library should seek to extend the normal statute of limitations for breach of contract (four years) because it often takes as many as five years to determine any defects in an automated library system or to determine its ability to meet the expected work load requirements.

What follows are recommended changes that the library should seek to be included in the newly drafted contract.

1. In order to preserve the library's flexibility should the automation project schedule fall behind, the contract should have a provision for allowing the library to change the delivery date of the system.

The library will have the right to change the attached delivery schedule without penalty, at any time, providing written notice is given to the vendor prior to the library having receipt of the vendor's two-week ship date notice.

This provision like all other obligations of either party, should be subject to "Force Majeure" that removes any penalty for ocurrences in schedule changes which are beyond a party's control, such as might be due in the case of fire, earthquake or flood.

2. As mentioned earlier, it is advisable to include in the contract, as attachments, the vendor's proposal response to the RFP, the vendor's promotional literature, and, if at all possible, the library's RFP. In addition, the actual contract should include the following three paragraphs that will provide

recourse to the library in the event that the automated library system does not perform as the library intended.

Vendor warrants all right, title and interest in the Library Automated System to the Library under this agreement. Further, vendor warrants that its right, title and interest to the Automated Library system to the Library under this agreement is free and clear of any lien, encumbrance or interest of any third party. Further, vendor warrants that it has the authority to grant the Library the rights provided to it by virtue of this agreement. Vendor warrants that the Automated Library System will perform in accordance with its noted functional and technical specifications (Attachment__) as well as with the performance criteria and representation indicated in any or all documentation that describes the Automated Library System and is attached hereto in Attachment _____.

Vendor warrants that during the first ninety (90) days after the Automated Library System has been accepted by the Library any defect in the System will be repaired or replaced without cost to the Library. Except as otherwise provided, all other warranties expressed or implied are disclaimed.

Vendor warrants that the Automated Library System herein descibed meets all appropriate OSHA safety and health requirements. Further, it warrants that the System will not produce or discharge in any manner or form, directly or indirectly, chemicals or toxic substances that could pose a hazard to the health or safety of anyone who may use or come in contact with the System, item, or matter produced by or through the System.

3. It may seem sensible that the library not assume responsibility or title to the Automated Library System until it is actually delivered into the library's premises. However, if the library accepts the vendor's shipping the equipment to the library FOB, the library, in fact, has accepted delivery of the System the moment it is handed over to a carrier, which may be many hundred miles away. To pursue the scenario further, if the carrier's truck or freightcar is involved in an accident and the System is damaged or destroyed, the library is liable for the System and must still pay the Vendor without ever having seen the automated library system. The only avenue open to the library to recoup its loss would be to sue the carrier and chase the insurer. The FOB clause can be handled in the following manner.

Vendor will deliver the Automated Library System "inside" at the Library's designated installation site. Risk of loss will not pass until such delivery has been completed in accordance with this provision.

Furthermore, the library should stipulate in the contract the criteria under which the automated system will be accepted and at what stage in the acceptance the title to the system will pass to the library. For example, it is advisable that the library not accept the system or assume title to the system until it has been uncrated, installed, and demonstrated by the vendor to be in working order. The demonstration might simply involve turning on the system and beginning the initial tape load of the library's holdings. The criteria for acceptance and the date of acceptance are critical and should be clearly specified in the contract so that the warranty period commences at that time. Otherwise the warranty period will begin automatically at the time the vendor installs the system. The following wording should appear in the contract in order to protect the library in these matters.

Upon receipt of Vendor's certificate that the Automated Library System is installed and in proper working order, the Library will initiate the first acceptance test.

The first acceptance test will consist of a tape load of the Library's bibliographic database. If the System performs in accordance with Vendor's performance specification (Attachment __) then the Library will accept title to the Automated Library System and make payment to the Vendor according to the schedule set forth in attachment _____. All warranties will commence from the date title passes to the Library.

Further liability for payment by the Library will be in accordance with provision _____ of this agreement.

The provision referenced in this last paragraph refers to additional acceptance testing that will be undertaken by the library before payment for the system is made. The nature and methods for running these tests were discussed in Chapter 4. The provision referred to above may carry the following wording in the contract.

No advance payment shall be made for goods or services furnished by vendor pursuant to this contract. All payments will be in accordance with the system acceptance tests described in attachment_____. Upon completion of installation of the System and upon completion of Equipment Certification, System Reliability, Functional Performance and Full-Load Response Time Acceptance Tests, Vendor will warrant in writing that the System is fit for the purpose.

5. Personnel training requirements from the RFP should be referenced in the contract. Additionally, it is advisable to require, via the contract, that the vendor certify in writing that staff are properly trained to use the system. This certification will protect the Library from the vendor sometime later backing away from liability by alleging that something went wrong with the System because staff was not properly trained. This may be taken one step further by the library in requiring that staff past a test on the operation of the System before accepting the Vendor's certification that training is complete. Of course, this option must be weighed against the effect on staff who may feel threatened by such a procedure. Possible wording for this part of the contract follows.

Vendor will provide training for the Library's personnel at no additional costs in accordance with the schedule indicated in attachment _. All such training will occur in accordance with a schedule mutually agreed upon by the parties and attached hereto. Vendor is aware that the Library cannot adequately test the System until the Vendor has issued a certicate indicating the Library's personnel are trained to operate the System so that it will function in accordance with the Vendor's performance specifications.

Vendor agrees that the Library's personnel will not have completed their training to operate the System until they have each been able to perform the functions stated in attachement _. Those employees who fail to perform those functions will be required to attend additional training sessions provided by the Vendor at no cost to the Library. These employees first will be required to complete the Vendor's efficiency tests to determine their eligibility for additional training on the system.

6. The library, via the contract, should take precautions to protect the Systems warranty period. If the warranty period begins while the system is down or continues when the system is unavailable due to a malfunction, the library could

miss the opportunity to put the System through its paces while still under warranty. A provision in the contract that extends the warranty period by the number of days the System was unavailable would solve this problem. Such a provision might read as follows.

In the event the Vendor repairs the System during the described warranty period in order to cure defects in the System's performance, then the described warranty period will be extended by the amount of time between when a defect was observed by the Library and its cure was completed by the Vendor, providing such period of time exceeds one (1) business day. This extension applies cumulatively and concurrently to any defects which arise during the said warranty period.

It is possible that after the warranty period has expired the System will be unavailable due to malfunctions time and time again. This obviously would present an unacceptable situation for the library and therefore should be addressed in the contract.

In addition to the contract clause which extends the warranty period, the contract should include an "insurance" provision. The provision would state that in the event the System is down a certain percent of the time, then it will be deemed ineffective for the purpose it was intended and the Vendor, in order to avoid a breach of contract, will have to replace the equipment within a specified period of time. A standard percentage of proficiency for automated library systems is 95%.

The provision should stipulate further that when the vendor replaces the system, the same acceptance testing procedures described in the acceptance provision would apply. Also, if the System is subsequently rejected, the library will pay on a rental basis only for the months the System was installed with the remainder of any purchase payments to be immediately refunded. Other penalties for failure to perform also would be invoked at this time. A suggested version of this contractual provision follows.

Regardless of the terms of the Maintenance Agreement herein, if the System fails to function in accordance with its respective performance specifications (therefore) stipulated in attachment _____ for a continuous period of _____ ( ) business days during any one (1) month, then the vendor will be obligated to replace the System immediately. The Library will have the right to "test" the new System according to the provisions set forth in attachment _____. The Library will have the right to reject the said replacement system if it fails to so conform, upon which all provisons of this agreement for failure to perform will be invoked.

7. The Library should amend the contract to protect itself from patent, copyright or trade secret infringement lawsuit. If the Library does not have such protection and is one day in an infringement case, the Library may have to pay the person or company that brought the infrigement action, not only for the right to use the System in the future, but also for the period of time in which the Library owned or leased the System. To avoid any infringement litigation the following language should appear in the contract.

Vendor warrants that the complete System provided to the Library under this agreement does not violate or infringe upon any third party interest based on a copyright, patent or trade secret.

In the event a third party asserts an interest against the Library's use, ownership or possession of the System alleging infringement or violation of a patent, copyright or trade secret, then the Library will so notifiy the Vendor who will immediately make every reasonable effort at its sole expense to secure for the Library the continued right to use the System without interference, but in any event will defend such claim in the Library's name at Vendor's sole cost and expense, saving the Library harm by paying any or all of the Library's fees, expenditures, damages or losses, to include but not limited to reasonable attorney's fees, (whether or not Vendor is successful) arising out of or relating to the claim for infringement.

The Library agrees to reasonably cooperate with the Vendor. However, the Vendor agrees not to settle any litigation in this matter without the express written permission of the Library. Reasonable cooperation does not extend to demands, which in the Library's reasonable opinion, impair its ability to conduct business.

This provision is separate, independent and exclusive from any other provision of this agreement. It is to be applied concurrently and consecutively with any other provision of this agreement.

90

8. While the Vendor usually is responsible for installing the automated library system, preparation of the site is the responsibility of the Library. The Vendor will provide to the Library the necessary specifications for electrical power, square footage, and climatic conditions (air conditions and humidity) necessary for the System to function properly. The Library will then hire a third party contractor to build the site according to the Vendor's specifications. In order to avoid the problem of the Vendor denying liability for a malfunction of the System, by alleging that the site was not prepared according to specifications, the Library, via the contract, should oblige the Vendor to inspect and certify that the site is suitable to support the System and will enable it to function according to the performance specifications established by the Library and the Vendor. The following wording should be used in the contract for this purpose.

Vendor has issued environmental specifications for the System here found in attachment _____. At its own expense, the Library will prepare the installation site for the System so that it will conform to the Vendor's environmental specifications. Forty-five (45) days prior to delivery of the System, the Library will notify the Vendor that the installation site has been so prepared and is ready for inspection; within five (5) business days after receipt of that notice (from the Library), Vendor will inspect the installation site to determine if it conforms to its environmental specifications. If it so conforms, the Vendor will issue a certificate indicating such conformity. If it fails to conform, the Vendor will list in writing each and every specific defect.

The Library will correct such defects within ten (10) buisness days and reinspection will occur within the next following five (5) business days. If there is conformity, the Vendor will issue its above noted certificate. If not, delivery will be delayed and rescheduled until after Vendor has certified in writing that the installation site conforms to its environmental specifications. If Vendor fails to inspect within the time frames of this provision, then it will be presumed that the installation site conforms to the Vendor's noted environmental specificaitions. Vendor acknowledges that the Library will reasonably and in good faith rely on that presumption.

9. Knowledge of obligatory and non-obligatory taxes is important in drafting the automation contract. Of course, if the library is a tax-free organization no taxes will be paid to the vendor. Even this should be clearly stated in the body

of the contract. If taxes are paid they are usually only those that flow from the use of the product. The vendor may try to make the library liable for taxes as if the vendor has ownership of the equipment. These taxes would then be in the form of excise taxes, franchise taxes, and personal property taxes. None of these taxes is the responsibility of the library.

If, on the other hand, the library is leasing the automated system, then certain taxes which flow from the vendor's ownership do apply to the library because the library will be using equipment in fact owned by the vendor. These taxes include sales taxes, use taxes, and personal property taxes.

Language that can be inserted into the automation contract might be:

The Library will pay only sales or use taxes arising directly from its acquisition or use of the automated library system. The library will have no other tax liability.

10. Important to be included in the automation contract are conditions for migrating the automated library system up to another system once it is outgrown by the library. This should include a complete trade-in schedule for all used equipment, database modification and loading, and all of the acceptance testing procedures outlined for the current system.

The vendor will repurchase the automated library system anytime within 5 years of the Library's acceptance of the system in accordance with the following repurchase schedule:

> *Within 2 years at 90% of purchase price*
> *Within 2 to 4 years at 65% of purchase price*
> *Within 4 to 5 years at 45% of purchase price*
> *After 5 years at 35% of purchase price*

Further, the vendor agrees to make all adjustments to the Library's databases necessary for their successful loading into the new automated library system. The Library will exercise the right to apply all acceptance criteria and methods described herein to the new automated library system.

Breach of Contract and Litigation. It almost always is undesirable for the Library to go to litigation over a breach of contract by the vendor. The money awarded seldom overrides incurred expense--assuming the courts rule in favor of the library.

The threat of suit by the library is often enough to get the vendor's attention and resume communication in an effective manner. The last thing that the vendor wants is a court battle, even if it thinks it would be successful, for fear of the negative publicity it would bring.

Nonetheless, in the event that the library chooses to bring the breach of contract to litigation, the following are concepts that will appear in any contract and should be understood by the library as it drafts the automation contract.

"Direct" damages are those caused directly by a breach of contract. "Consequential" damages are those losses resulting from the direct damages. "Incidental" damages are those expenses incurred in using products or services to lessen the losses caused by breach of contract.

NEGOTIATING THE CONTRACT

Protecting the interests of the library as it ventures into the acquisition of an automated library system means the following.

o That the automated system perform as represented in the vendors proposal

o That the vendor provide the support necessary to implement and maintain the system successfully

o That fixes of the system occur quickly, especially during the warranty period

o That payment be withheld until the system works properly

o That the vendor guarantee safe delivery of the system and the library not be required to accept any equipment damaged during transport

o That the library not be responsible for any additional costs beyond those initially agreed to o That the staff be properly trained by the vendor in the operation and maintenance of the system

As it has been pointed out, the vendor's standard contract seldom protects these interests and therefore must be re-drafted by the library. It is of primary importance that the library know it's negotiating strength and also know that while some vendors will negotiate all of the time and all vendors will negotiate some of the time, no vendor will refuse to negotiate all of the time.

Negotiating strength comes from a number of variables called leverage. The library's leverage depends on a number of factors: its size and reputation; the amount of equipment or the size of the system being purchased; whether or not the library will serve the vendor as a "Beta Site" (test or pilot site) for a system newly introduced into the marketplace; the ability and willingness for the library to "sell" by example other libraries in its region on a particular automated library system.

It would be unrealistic, however, to assume that all vendors looking for your library's business will negotiate to the same degree in making contractual concessions. As discussed in Chapter 3, one method of determining which vendor is most willing to negotiate is by inserting questions into the RFP concerning the vendors posture on certain contract terms and conditions.

The first step to successful contract negotiation is knowing the proper roles of each member of the negotiating teams, the library's and the vendor's. It is inevitable that the first person within the vendor's organization that the library will come into contact with will be the sales representative. While this person may be a degreed librarian, it is essential to understand that as an employee of a for-profit organization he or she will be well versed in the skills of sales. The principle objective of this individual is to sell the system and to "cut the deal". While this is an expected role for the sales representative to play, the library must, nevertheless, exercise control over the dynamics that will come into play between the sale representative and the library. If the library loses control, two unacceptable things will happen: first, the representative will redefine the library's automation requirements to mesh more closely with the automated system the particular vendor is marketing, and second, the library's ability to negotiate the most favorable contract to the library will be curtailed.

To maintain control from the outset of the relationship, the library must be confident in its automation requirements, as set out in the RFP, and understand that the sales representative does not have the authority to apply changes to the automation contract. For this reason it is important, as early as possible, to find out from the sales representative the name of the person who does have contract-changing authority. This is the individual to whom the library should target it's negotiation.

To avoid leaving the reader with a false impression concerning the role of the sales representative, it should be stated that in most cases this individual is a highly trained professional who understands library operations and the nature of library automation requirements. The sales representative is probably the person who actually drafted the vendor's proposal and who is most familiar with the library's RFP. For the acquisition process to have reached the contract negotiating stage, the sales representative should, at this point, be commended for his or her talents in understanding the library's automation needs and translating them into the vendor's ability to meet them.

While the sales representative will in most cases continue as a member of the vendor's negotiating team, his or her role in helping the library achieve a contract that is in the best interests of the library has diminished. This situation must be recognized by the library.

As a preliminary strategy for negotiating a successful contract, the members of the library's negotiating team, as well as the library administration must provide a united front. Otherwise the vendor representatives will sieze the opportunity to approach individual library administrators and members of the negotiating team in an attempt to persuade them toward their point of view in the hope that peer presure and majority sentiment will lessen the amount or degree of concessions the library is seeking from the vendor. Internal discipline of library staff and agreement that there is one and only one individual on the library's negotiating team authorized to make decisions during the negotiation process is very important. Negotiation process is here defined as that time in which the parties to the contract are sitting around a table debating the concessions the vendor will and will not make concerning the automation contract. Prior to entering into the negotiation process the library's negotiating team should have agreed upon a list of contract priorities. The contract changes which the library is asking the vendor to agree to should be presented one at a time in reverse priority order. The strategy here is that the library will convey the initial feeling that what is being requested is reasonable and should be easily acceptable to the vendor. Also, it allows for early agreement to be reached on a number of areas, which at a later time can be offered by the library as sacrifices in order to obtain agreement on those items which truly are important to the library.

Members of the library's negotiating team may typically include the project director, a member of the library's top administration, a library automation consultant and the library's legal representative. It is advisable to include legal counsel only if the vendor includes in their negotiating team a counter-part. The fees paid to the attorney are better reserved to pay for legal review of the contract after it has been negotiated and before it is signed by the library.

A strategy for successful contract negotiation is the development of a formal agenda for each important bargaining session. Such a strategy has several advantages.

First, it forces the library's negotiating team to review its priorities, goals, and objectives in the context of a particular barganining session. Even if the desired outcomes from the session have been well rehersed by the team, often the individual members of the team are only generally aware of the points or questions they intend to cover at a particular meeting. Also, many times they have given little or no thought to the order of the meeting or the psychological advantages that might be obtained by bringing issues up in a particular fashion.

Second, an agenda strengthens the ability of the library to control the negotiation process, and thereby, enhances the ability to accomplish its own objectives. Control of the negotiation session can be critical in disrupting any number of the vendor's negotiating ploys.

As experienced negotiators, some vendors will attempt to disconnect related issues in order to reach agreement on a single non-controversial matter while deferring its related controversial component to a later time. This will enable the vendor, at a later time, when the deferred item surfaces, to allege surprise because the library has already agreed to the companion item. The library's ability to achieve negotiating success is related to its skill in controlling the order in which issues are discussed and to present related issues together.

Third, an agenda will generally catch the vendor off balance. Most vendors will be surprised that the library had the forthought to prepare a negotiating agenda and will, as a result, be immediately put on the defensive by the act. It gives the library the psychological advantage and if accepted by the vendor gives the library its first victory.

Fourth, the agenda serves as a vehicle to reinforce the concerns of the library as expressed in its RFP. It obligates the vendor to acknowledge the importance of the library's concerns and becomes a subtle tool to implement the library's negotiating strategy.

The following is an example of a negotiating agenda broken down into three sessions. The reader should take note that the points included in the agenda are only examples and should be modified to the specific library. (Adapted from *EDP Solutions*, 1984).

SESSION I

I. Meeting Arrangements and Schedule

    A. Introductions
    B. Ground Rules
    C. Negotiation Objectives
        1. Vendor intentions/needs
        2. Library intentions/needs
    D. Agenda Review
    E. Agreement Potential

II. Vendor Representations and Commitments
    A. Vendor's Presentation of Its "Deliverables"
        1. Inclusion of Vendor Proposal in Contract--penalties
        2. Incl sion of Benchmark Results in Contract--penalties
        3. Acceptance Tests--penalties
            a. Hardware
            b. Software--Operating
            c. Software--Application

4. Ongoing Performance Criteria--penalties
   a. Maintenance
   b. System Support
   c. Hardware--Current and Future
   d. Operating Software--Current and Future--
     Revisions
   e. Application Software

B. Library's Explanation of Its Concerns (If any)
  1. Resolution of Concerns (If possible)
  2. No Resolution--Co±tinuation Decision by
  Library (If applicable)

C. Agreement on Vendor's Ability to Perform
  (Including Warranties and Remedies Acceptable
  to Library)

III. Break--Caucus--Library Continuation Decision Work Session (If applicable)

SESSION II

I. Vendor Payment Aspirations
  A. Review of Vendor Concessions
  B. Review of Payment Schedule versus Library
    Risks (at various timeframes)

II. Caucus--Library Continuation Decision--Meeting
  Resumption (If applicable)

III. Vendor's Ability to Meet Library's Critial Needs
  A. MARC Input and Output
  B. 98% Up-time Rate
  C. Emergency Hardware Replacement
  D. Delivery Standards and Detailed Installation
    Plan
  E. Damages for Late Delivery, Installation or
    Acceptance
  F. Free Documentation Copies

G. Certification of Training to Staff

H. Performance Bond

I. Price Warranty

IV. Caucus--User Continuation Decision--Meeting Resumption (If applicable)

V. Vendor's Presentation of Contractual Documents to Substantiate Vendor's Representations

A. Presentation and Review of Documents by Vendor's Counsel

B. Comment by Library's Counsel

C. Conceptual Agreement (If possible)

D. Assignment of Drafting Responsibilites and Completion Dates

SESSION III

I. Review Remaining Tasks, Responsibilites and Timeframes

II. Review Points of Agreement and Consider any Remaining Problems

III. Schedule Contract Signing or Outline Objectives for Next Meeting

Beyond developing an agenda, the library also can exercise control over the negotiation process by selecting the time and place of the negotiation sessions. Most individuals have certain periods during the day when they perform best. By assessing the library team's preference and selecting the majority period, the library will maximize it's negotiating effectiveness. The place in which the negotiation will be held is usually determined by the library. The selection of the site should depend on where it is that the team feels it can optimize control over the bargaining process. It can be in a hotel suite, arranged informally around a bright sitting room, a formal conference room, or a dingy, cramped room with uncomfortable furniture. There are few rules of thumb for selecting the negotiating site. The best that can be said is that the site should complement the strategy for negotiating the contract. Often this simply means that the home court with its familiarity and convenience will be the most advantageous. It will allow the library to control many critical factors such as travel, food, fatigue and physical surroundings.

ONGOING MANAGEMENT OF THE AUTOMATED SYSTEM

Library automation carries with it a life cycle that must be managed on a continuous basis. The life cycle includes the following phases (Noland, 1976).

Initiation. The automated system is installed and tested. All aspects of this stage, as with every stage, must be documented. Management's responsibility is to ascertain the degree to which the objectives of the automated system have been achieved. Evaluation of system performance, and training effectiveness also is an important management activity within this stage of the system's life-cycle. It is in this first stage that managment should seek ways to control quality. Quality control is achieved by predetermining standards for the automated system's outputs. These standards are based on thresholds of acceptability, which are attained by examining the end-user's requirements. A priority rating can be assigned to each output in accordance with its importance to the end-user. Each output is rated on a scale of one to four, one being that the output is less than acceptable, and four that it is more than acceptable. This value, multiplied by the priority rating, gives each output a weighted score when evaluated. Because management is interested in evaluating the quality of the overall system in the context of cost, it is necessary to divide the cost by the total score. The result is a cost/performance evaluation. This method of measuring and controlling quality of the automated system is demonstrated in Figures 4.1 and 4.2.

Formalization. Controls are introduced by managment to ensure efficient operation of the automated library system. Manual procedures have been fully meshed with the automation procedures, all program "bugs" have been resolved, and staff have been trained thoroughly with an on-going training program in place. It is in this stage of the system life-cycle that the library and vendor develops a comfortable working relationship, where the channels of communication have become fully effective and there are few surprises accompanying the operation and management of the automated library system.

Expansion. Monitoring work load requirements are essential in order to anticipate the addition of storage space, terminals and other peripheral equipment that may have been identified as part of the growth requirements for the automated system. These growth requirements should be within the parameters outlined in the automation contract and thereby of no surprise to the library or vendor. It is for this reason that careful attention was given to calculating future workload requirements.

In addition to this activity management has the responsibility of evaluating the need for expansion beyond what was initially anticipated. The development of new applications and technology provide opportunity for expansion. Management must emphasize control in the stage of the life-cycle, particularly with costs. Staff and patrons at this stage have adapted fully to the automated system and are looking anxiously for additional technological innovations without any real examination of costs. This technological fascination can result in the acquisition of enhancements to the automated library system that have few real benefits to service or operating efficiency. Management is faced with a delicate balancing task. As technology advances, there are considerable advantages in keeping up with the state of the art--faster systems, more capabilities, improved efficiency. At the same time, it must not allow the expansion to get out of control.

Maturity. The library organization has integrated an automation program in its future development. The structure and staff of the library are completely supportive of automation, and cost efficient enhancements to the automated library system are sought. It is in this last stage of the life-cycle that the library prepares to migrate to a larger automated system. Management consolidates documents and experiences in order to evaluate the future needs for automation. The contagious outbreak for innovative technology by staff and patrons is managed carefully in order to seek new revenue for automation and to identify the most effective options for entering into a new library automation life-cycle.

On-going management of the automated library system means that the library's management has assumed a new expanded role for integrating automation into the organizational structure and operations of the library. It is an activity that will influence all aspects of library service and provide an opportunity to explore new and challenging ways to expand service.

REFERENCE

EDP Solutions. Delran, NJ: Datapro Research Corporation, 1984.

Noland, R. L., "Business Needs a New Kind of EDP Manager," *Harvard Business Review,* 57 (1976), 123-33.

APPENDIX A

SELECTED LIST OF TURNKEY VENDORS

Carlyle Systems Inc., 2930 San Pablo Avenue, Berkeley CA 94702, (415) 843-3538.

CLSI, 1220 Washington Street, West Newton MA 02165, (617) 965-6310.

Comstow Information Services, 302 Boxboro Road, Stow MA 01775, (617) 897-7163.

DTI Data Trek, 621 Second Street, Encinitas CA 92024, (619) 436-5055.

Dahlgren Memorial Library, Georgetown University Medical Center, 3900 Reservoir Road, Washington DC 20007, (202) 625-7673.

Data Research Associates, Inc., 9270 Olive Boulevard, St. Louis MO 63132-3276 (314) 432-1100.

Dynix, 1455 West 820 North, Provo UT 84601, (801) 375-2770.

Electric Memory Inc., 656 Munras Avenue, P.O. Box 1439, Monterey CA 93942, (408) 646-9666.

Eyring Research Institute, 5280 South 320 West, Suite E260, Salt Lake City UT 84107, (801) 263-9200.

Gaylord Systems Division, Box 4901, Syracuse NY 13221, (800) 448-6160.

Geac, 350 Steelcase Road West, Markham, Ontario L3R 1B3, Canada, (416) 475-0525.

IBM Academic Information Systems, 472 Wheelers Farms Road, Milford CT 06460, (203) 783-7385.

INLEX, P.O. Box 1349, Monterey, CA 93942, (408) 646-9666.

Info-Doc. Box 17109, Dulles International Airport, Washington DC 20041, (800) 336-0800/(703) 486-0900.

Innovative Interfaces, Inc., 1409 Fifth Street, Berkeley CA 94710, (415) 527-5555.

LIAS Program Office, E-1 Pattee Library, University Park PA 16802, (814) 865-1818.

Library Information Systems, Inc. 840 Irvine Avenue, Suite S-210, Newport Beach CA 92663, (714) 631-0784.

M/A-COM Information Systems, Inc., 5515 Security Lane, Rockville MD 20852, (301) 984-3636.

McLeod-Bishop Systems Ltd., 1600 Carling Avenue, #400, Ottawa, Ontario K1Z 8R7, Canada, (613) 728-7781.

Northwestern University Library, 1935 Sheridan Road, Evanston IL 60201, (312) 492-7004.

OCLC Inc., Local Systems Division, 6565 Frantz Road, Dublin OH 43017-0702, (614) 764-6000.

Sedna Corporation, 970 Raymond Avenue, St. Paul MN 55114, (612) 647-1101.

Sirsi Corporation, 8106-B South Memorial Parkway, Huntsville AL 35802, (205) 881-2140.

Sperry Corporation Computer Systems, P.O. Box 500, Blue Bell PA 19424-0001, (215) 542-4312.

Sydney Dataproducts Inc., 11075 Santa Monica Boulevard, Suite 100, Los Angeles CA 90025, (213) 479-4621.

Systems Control, Inc., Commercial and Industrial Systems, P.O. Box 10025, Palo Alto CA 94303, (415) 494-1165.

Universal Library Systems, 205-1571 Bellevue Avenue, West Vancouver, British Columbia V7V 1A6, Canada, (604) 926-7421.

UTLAS Corp., 701 Westchester Avenue, Suite 308W, White Plains NY 10604, (914) 997-1495.

Virginia Tech, Center for Library Automation, 416 Newman Library, Blacksburg VA 24061, (703) 961-6452.

Washington University School of Medicine Library, 4580 Scott Avenue, St. Louis MO 63110, (314) 454-3711.

SOURCES FOR CANDIDATE SYSTEMS INFORMATION

Directory of Information Management Software for Libraries, Information Centers, and Record Centers. Edited by Pamela Cibbarelli and Edward Kazlauskas. Annual. $49.00. Available from Pacific Information Inc., 11684 Ventura Blvd., Suite 295, Studio City, CA 91604. Describes over 125 packages useful for library automation. Covers mainframes, minicomputers, and microcomputers. Indexed by application, hardware, component. (Also available from the American Library Association.)

Library Systems Evaluation Guides. Powell, OH: James E. Rush Associates. Projected 8 volume set at $395.00. Single volumes on individual topics available at $59.50. A guide to a comprehensive method of evaluating library automation support. Provides an inventory of available systems.

Library Systems Newsletter. Chicago, IL: Library Technology Reports, American Library Association. Individual issues of the Newsletter are devoted to an "Annual Review of Supported Software Vendors."

APPENDIX B

Example of Functional Specifications

FUNCTIONAL SPECIFICATIONS

Charge Function

Definition: a procedure by which a library loans an
item or items from its collection to an eligible
borrower for a specified length of time.

Library staff must be able to charge out items to a
borrower by optically scanning with an optical input
device a unique identifier on the borrower's card and a
unique identifier on each item to be charged out. The
system must also accept input of the unique identifiers
by keying. These inputs must be supported by full
online borrower, title, and item files. The system
must provide audible and visual signals to indicate
successful completion of a normal charge transaction.

The system must be able to charge out items to special
borrowers (bindery, missing, mending, etc.)

The system must automatically choose the appropriate
loan period based on the category of borrower and the
type and format of item.

The system must be designed so that the due date may be
set automatically either by interval (i.e., the due
date is three weeks from date of charge) or by fixed
date (i.e., all items charged out during an academic
quarter are due on the same date at the end of the
quarter). It must be possible to use both methods
simultaneously or only one method. It must be possible
to set interval due dates automatically by hours, days,
weeks, or months. It must be possible to modify the
schedule of due dates easily, without programmer
intervention.

The system must avoid using certain library-specified
days as due dates. _____ must be able to have a unique
schedule of ineligible due dates, and this schedule
must be asily modifiable without programmer

intervention.

The system must allow authorized library staff to set a due date different from that selected by the system for any item or borrower.

The system must not display borrower data as a result of entering the borrower unique identifier for a normal charge transaction.

The system must not display item data as a result of entering the item unique identifier for a normal charge transaction.

System software must be designed so that, when charging out several items to a single borrower, the borrower unique identifier need be entered only once.

Some process must be provided to prevent library staff from charging out items to one borrower on a previous borrower's unique identifier.

Library staff must be able to use the system to circulate items that are not cataloged or fully processed by entering a temporary brief bibliographic record for the item and assigning to the record a randomly selected item unique identifier.

If an item presented for charge by a borrower was never discharged, the system must automaticaly discharge it, flag the item record, and continue the charge transaction. The system must have the capability to produce, on demand, a report which lists these items.

The Charge Function must occur in real time for all transactions.

The system must not have the capability to maintain a historical list of items charged out by a particular borrower beyond requirements for file backup.

Audible and visual signals, easily distinguishable from normal transaction signals, must be provided by the system and the system must interrupt the charge transaction when:

-- there is no record in the borrower file for the borrower unique identifier entered;

-- there is no record in the item file for the item unique identifier entered;

-- the item is noncirculating;

-- the borrower is delinquent;

-- there is a hold on the item;

-- the loan period specified by library staff exceeds a specified time period;

-- the item has a status other than "on shelf;"

-- the borrower unique identifier entered corresponds to a borrower card that has been cancelled or reported lost or stolen;

-- the borrower has a message, e.g., "hold" book at desk.

The system must display information in detail about which of the above conditions caused the charge transaction to be interrupted. The system must allow authorized library staff to continue the charge transaction after entering a password.

The system must give the highest priority to the Charge Function and must maintain a response time of less than two (2) seconds for all charge transactions.

It must be possible to charge items to a borrower on the borrower's first visit to the library.

The system must not assign due dates later than the expiration date of the borrower's card.

Renewal Function

Definition: a procedure by which a library extends the due date of an item already charged out to a borrower.

All functional specifications described under Charge

Function apply to the Renewal Function, except that it is <u>not</u> required that the item unique identifier be entered to accomplish renewal, and a status of "missing" or "lost" must not cause the renewal transaction to be interrupted.

The system must automatically extend the due date of an item that is charged out when library staff enter the borrower unique identifier, either by scanning or keying, and indicate in some manner the item to one renewed. It is required that it not be necessary to enter both the borrower unique identifer and the item unique identifier to accomplish renewal.

It must be possible to automatically limit renewals of individual items to a specified number. This number must be easily changeable without programmer intervention.

Audible and visual signals, easily distinguishable from normal transaction signals, must be provided by the system and the system must interrupt the renewal transaction when:

-- the item has already been renewed the maximum number of times permitted;

-- the item is overdue beyond a _____ specified threshold.

The system must display information in detail about which of the above conditions caused the renewal transaction to be interrupted. The system must allow authorized library staff to continue the renewal transaction after entering a password. The system must not assign due dates later than the expiration date of the borrower's card.

Discharge Function

Definition: a procedure by which a library removes an item from charged status and breaks the link between the item and the borrower.

Library staff must be able to discharge items by entering, either by scanning or keying, the it m unique identifier; the item unique identifier must be the only input to this function.

If the discharge transaction is occurring on or before the due date, the system must break the link between the borrower and the item upon input of the item unique identifier and set the item status either to "on shelf" or "en route". The system must provide audible and visual signals to indicate successful completion of the discharge transaction.

If the discharge transaction is occurring after the due date, the system must immediately tabulate and record in the borrower's account all fines and/or service charges associated with the item being discharged, if this has not already been done, and must allow the item to be immediately circulated by another borrower.

If a replacement charge has been levied for an overdue item by the time of the discharge transaction for that item, the system must automatically delete the replacement charge, if it has not already been paid, from the borrower's account while leaving other fines/service charges unaffected.

Authorized library staff must be able to assign a fee in any amount to a borrower's account and specify a reason for the fee (e.g., if a book was returned damaged and had to be rebound) after entering a password.

The system must not break the link between the borrower and an item as long as there are unpaid fines/service charges associated with that item.

The Discharge Function must occur in real time for all transactions.

If the item being discharged is assigned to a location other than the one in which the discharge transaction is taking place, the system must discharge the item, set the item status to "en route," provide an audible signal distinct from the normal transaction signal, and display information about the proper location of the item. The display should be in such a format that, if printed on a printer connected to the terminal, the resulting printout could be used as a routing slip for returning the item to its proper location. The displayed information must include at least the item title, call number, unique identifier, destination library, and current date. If the item has been assigned to a temporary location, it is this temporary location that must govern whether or not the item receives "en route" status, and the location information displayed must pertain to a temporary location.

If the item unique identifier for an item with a status of "en route" is entered under the Discharge Function, the system must automatically change the item status to "on shelf."

Audible and visual signals, easily distinguishable from normal transaction signals, must be provided by the system and the system must interrupt the discharge transaction when:

-- there is no item record for the item unique identifier entered;

-- the item has a status other than "charged out," "en route," or "missing;"

-- there is a hold on the item;

-- the item is booked to be shipped or picked up within 48 hours of discharge.

The system must display information in detail about which of the above conditions caused the discharge transaction to be interrrupted. The system must allow authorized library staff to continue the discharge transaction after entering a password.

If an item being discharged is represented in the data base only by a temporary brief bibliographic record, the system must automaticaly delete the temporary brief bibliographic record as a result of a successful discharge transaction. The system must provide audible and visual signals, easily distinguishable from normal transaction signals, to indicate to library staff that the item may need special handling.

APPENDIX B / FUNCTIONAL SPECIFICATIONS

Overdue/Fine Function.

Definition: a procedure by which the library notifies borrowers that they have overdue items from the library and computes fines against borrowers according to a set policy.

_____ must be able to easily modify fine/service charge and overdue notification parameters without programmer intervention.

The system must have the capability to automatically levy fines/service charges in at least two ways:

-- an accumulating fine levied hourly, daily, weekly, or monthly, based on the open hours of the lending branch and the format of the item (periodicals, books, etc.).

-- a service charge (fixed amount) levied a library-specified amount of time after the due date.

Each branch must be able to use either or both methods.

The system must allow authorized library staff to enter charges in any amount on a borrower's account after entering a password; it must also be possible to enter a reason for the fine/service charge.

The system must automatically produce overdue notices in zipcode order at _____ specified intervals after the due date and on demand. The intervals must be easily modifiable without programmer intervention.

The system must have the capability to add, subtract, and display itemized accounts and totals for the fines/service charges in a borrower's account.

The system must be able to accept full, partial, or no payment of monies. The system must allow authorized library staff, after entering a password, to delete all or part of the fines/service charges on a borrower's account. The system must maintain a record of transactions that have been deleted.

The system must not break the link between an item and a borrower as long as there are unpaid fines/service charges associated with that item.

The system must automatically set the borrower's status to "delinquent" if:

-- the borrower has unpaid fines/service charges beyond a _____ specifed threshold;

-- the borrower has items overdue a length of time which exceeds a _____ specified threshold;

-- the borrower has been inactive for a _____ specifed period of time;

-- the borrower's use of the "claims returned" status or the "reported lost" status exceeds a _____ specified threshold;

The thresholds must be easily modifiable without programmer intervention.

It must be possible for authorized library staff, after entering a password, to set a borrower's status to "delinquent."

The system must have the capability to automatically set an overdue item's status to "missing" and then to "lost" at _____ specified intervals. The intervals must be easily modifiable without programmer intervention.

The system must have the capability to automatically levy a replacement charge on the borrower's account whenever an item charged to that borrower is assigned, either by the system or by library staff, a status of "missing." The amount of the replacement charge must be obtained by the system either from price information in the bibliographic record for the item or from an average price table if there is no price information in the bibliographic record. It must be possible to easily modify the table without programmer intervention.

The system must have the capability to calculate the
fine to that point when the patron reports that an item
is lost. When the branch flags the item as lost, the
fine calculations should be performed automatically as
of date reported lost and retained until the fine is
cleared.

The system must have the capability to calculate the
fine if the item is overdue and not returned to the
owning branch.

The system must have the capability to automatically
produce a bill which shows all unpaid fines/service
charges owed by a borrower whenever an item charged to
that borrower is declared missing. The system must
also have the capability to produce such a bill on
demand regardless of the item status.

The system must have the capability to determine and
display the category of the borrower.

Authorized library staff must be able to determine
instantly, via terminal display, a borrower's status,
items charged to a borrower that are overdue, and
fines/service charges (itemized) owed by a borrower.

If a borrower claims to have returned an item
for which s/he is being assessed a replacement charge,
it must be possible for library staff to set the item
status to "claims returned" and to delete the
replacement charge. The system must keep a tally of
the number of times each borrower uses the "claims
returned" status.

It must be possible for authorized staff to set
item status to "reported lost."

The system must inhibit the production of overdue
notices for items with a status of "claims returned" or
"reported lost."

Notice Function

Definition: notices are used by a library to alert
borrowers to possession of overdue books, to holds being
satisfied, to unpaid fines, etc.

APPENDIX B / FUNCTIONAL SPECIFICATIONS

The system must have the capability to produce printed notices in batch runs at the CPU site. _____ must be able to have a unique schedule and profile for notices, both as to parameters for notice production and as to which notices are used. These schedules and parameters must be easily modifiable without programmer intervention. Each vendor must supply with the proposal samples of all standard notices produced by the proposed system and indicate the degree of flexibility available to _____ in reformatting the notices.

All notices must be produced on postcard stock in zip code order in a batch run at the CPU site. All notices must have printed on them the borrower's name and address in mailing format acceptable to the U.S. Postal Service. Additional information that is required for each type of notice is specified below.

-- Availability notice (Hold Function): item title, item call number, item unique identifier, statement that item is available for charge, member and branch name which is pickup location, current date.

-- Cancellation notice (Hold Function): item title, item call number, item unique identifier, statement that hold is cancelled, reason for cancellation, member and branch name, current date.

-- First and second overdue and/or reminder notices (Overdue/Fine Function): item title(s), item call number(s), item unique identifier(s), statement that item(s) is overdue, branch name, the second notice should accommodate at least to five items and list charges.

-- Damage notice (Items found to be damaged after return): item title, item calll number, item unique identifier, statement hat item is damaged, type of damage, charges for damage, and branch.

116

APPENDIX B / FUNCTIONAL SPECIFICATIONS
APPENDIX B / FUNCTIONAL SPECIFICATIONS

The system must inhibit the sending of overdue notices for items with a status of "claims returned" or "reported lost."

The system must have the capability to produce a bill which shows those fines/service charges associated with a borrower's activity. The bill must have an itemized list of the fines/service charges owed and the total amount. Bills must be produced in a batch run at the CPU site in zip code order and counted for bulk mail permit. The system should employ the technique of "crash printing" (i.e., printing on forms through envelopes) in order to eliminate the need to stuff envelopes. If the proposed system does not use this technique, the bill format must be suitable for insertion in a window envelope. Name and address format must conform to U.S. Postal Service requirements. For each fine owed, the bill must show the item title, item call number, and the item unique identifier. Other information that is required includes due date of payment, statement of consequences of failure to pay, member and branch name, and current date.

All items must be counted by computer for bulk mailing.

Purge Function

Definition: the ability to have the data base purged of designated items, and a print-out of such items produced.

The system must purge items from the borrower's file when specified by _____ as follows:

- -- by expiration date of borrower's card
- -- by last activity of borrower
- -- by patron category
- -- by amount and/or listing of fines outstanding over a designated period of time.

Branch-to-Branch Transfer

Definition: a procedure by which an item is temporarily loaned by one branch library to another branch library.

The ability to change a block of items from one branch location to another merely by scanning their item unique identifiers is required.

The ability to change a single item from one branch location to another merely by scanning their item unique identifiers is required.

The ability to automatically alert the borrowing library when item(s) should be returned to the lending library is required.

Reserve Book Room Function

Definition: usually in an academic library, a procedure by which the library removes an item from general circulation and makes it available only on a restricted basis.

The system must allow library staff to designate an item as a reserve book room item by establishing a link between the item and a course or faculty member. Establishment of this link must be a distinct function from the normal charge function, and it must be possible to circulate a reserve book room item to borrowers using the normal charge function.

The system should accept holds on reserve book room items. Placement of a hold on a reserve book room item should not affect the due date or time or cause production of a recall notice.

The system must be able to assess fines/service charges on an hourly basis. The system must keep track of when the library is closed and not assess fines during closed hours for reserve book room items.

The system must be able to produce daily overdue notices for overdue reserve book room items.

It must be possible to access the title/item file by course name and faculty member name for reserve book room items and obtain a display of items linked to the course or faculty member specified.

For each reserve book room item, it must be possible to specify a clear date, and the system must have the capability to produce a printed report listing, in call number order, items having a given clear date. The clear date is the date the item is to be returned to the general collection.

Hold Function

Definition: a procedure by which the library reserves for a borrower the right to charge out, before any other borrower, an item that is currently unavailable for charge.

Library staff must be able to place a hold on an item by entering, scanning or keying the borrower unique identifier and indicating in some manner the object of the hold. The system must provide audible and visual signals to indicate successful completion of the hold transaction, and set item status to "on hold."

The system must accept a hold against all copies of a title (title-specific hold), all copies of an edition (edition-specific hold), and against a specific copy (copy-specific hold).

The system must have the capability to make any item in any _____ library available to the borrower regardless of which branch library it is housed in. When a hold is placed on a title, all copies should be tagged so that the first copy available will be sent to the borrower. If there is more than one request in the hold queue, the requests must be filled sequentially (first in, first out).

In other words, if, at the time a hold is entered for an item (title-, edition-, or copy-specific), no copy is available in any location, the system must establish a hold queue. The order of the hold queue must be the chronological order in which the holds were placed.

The system must allow library staff to specify a pickup location (i.e., a different branch library) other than the location (branch library) where the hold is placed. The system must default to the branch library where the hold is placed if no alternative is specifed.

Whenever an item is trapped by the system due to a hold, it is desirable that library staff be able to charge the item immediately to the first borrower in the hold queue, without having to enter the borrower unique identifier or change to the Charge Function. The period which the item will be held for a patron must be limited to a specific length of time which can be modified without the intervention of a programmer.

The system must allow library staff to specify an expiration date for a hold. On the expiration date, if the item has not been charged out or the hold cancelled, the system must automatically cancel the hold. If a hold queue exists for the item, the system must have the capability to automatically produce a notice of availability for the next borrower in the queue. If no expiration date is specified, the hold must be maintained indefinitely.

It must be possible for authorized library staff to alter the order of the hold queue after entering a password.

The queue algorithm which determines which borrower should get the next available copy of a title should take into account both holds on titles and holds on specific copies of a title. Each vendor must specify in the proposal the algorithm used in the proposed system and how it weights two demands on the same item.

The system must automatically detect when an item with a hold on it becomes available for charge and provide audible and visual signals to library staff without regard for the location of the item, the branch library, the borrower, or the function underway at the time. The audible signal must be easily distinguishable from a normal transaction signal. The visual display should contain sufficient information and be formatted in such a way that, if printed on a printer connected to the terminal, the resulting printout could function as a routing slip or mailing label. The borrower information displayed must correspond to the first borrower in the hold queue. The system must have the capability to automatically produce a notice of availability for the first borrower in the hold queue.

When an item is charged to a borrower who has a hold on
the item, the system must automatically delete that
hold from the hold queue.

The system must not satisfy a hold with an item which
is on interlibrary loan from another library.

When a hold is placed on an item that is charged out on
a normal charge and for which no hold queue exists, the
system must have the capability to automatically reset
the due date to a specified number of days from the
date of the hold unless the original due date is
already within the specified number of days from the
date of the hold transaction, in which case the due
date is not altered. In either case, the system must
automatically produce a recall notice which alerts the
current borrower that the item has a new due date, if
it does, and is on hold.

If, at the time the hold is placed, there is a hold
queue for the item, or the item is a reserve book room
item, the system must not alter the due date or produce
a recall notice.

Library staff must be able to determine instantly, via
terminal display, the position of a borrower in a hold
queue.

Authorized library staff must be able to manually cancel
any hold. It should be possible for authorized
library staff to cancel all holds on an item or title
by entering a single command after entering a
password.

The system should automatically transfer all holds to
other copies for items with a status of "claims
returned," "reported lost," "lost," and "missing." If
the item is a final copy, a list of the items that are
missing, with complete bibliographic information
(author, title, publisher, date, ISBN#), and a list of
patrons with holds on the item, should be generated so
replacement copies can be purchased.

For each hold that is cancelled, whether automatically
or manually, the system must have the capability to

produce a cancellation notice.

The system must have the capability to produce a report which identifies those items with a specified ratio of holds to copies for _____ as a whole. Under password control each branch must be able to specify a different ratio and to easily change the ratio without programmer intervention.

The file updates associated with the Hold Function must be done in real time.

The system must provide audible and visual signals, easily distinguishable from normal transaction signals, and must interrupt the hold transaction when:

-- there is no record for the borrower unique identifier entered;

-- the borrower already has a hold on the item indicated;

-- the item is one which must be booked for use.

The system must provide information in detail about which of the above conditions caused the hold transaction to be interrupted. Authorized library staff must be able to continue the hold transaction after entering a password, except that it must not be possible to place a hold on an item which must be booked for use.

The system must provide at least a two level item status, so that, for example, an item may have, simultaneously, a status of "charged out" and a status of "on hold."

Booking Function

Definition: a procedure, used only with specifically designated materials, by which a library can reserve or "book" an item(s) for a borrower for use on a specific date and during a specific period of time.

Library staff must be able to book an item by entering the borrower unique identifier and the item unique

identifier by scanning or keying and specifying the
date and time of the booking. The system must provide
audible and visual signals to indicate successful
completion of the book transaction.

The system must allow only certain specifically
designated materials to be booked.

Library staff must be able to specify a date that an
item needs to be shipped, the address to which it needs
to be shipped, and special shipping instructions, in
addition to the regular booking information.

Library staff must be able to specify a pickup location
other than the member and branch where the item is
located. If a date of shipment or a pickup location is
not specified, the system must default to a pickup
location of the member and branch where the item is
currently located.

It must be possible to book more than one item for a
single borrower without having to re-enter the borrower
unique identifier for each item.

The system must automatically prevent specification of
a pickup date or shipment date that occurs when the
member/branch will be closed.

The Booking Function should be supported by the same
on-line borrower, title, and item files as all other
functions. It should not be necessary to create
separate borrower, title, or item files for this
function.

The system must have the capability to display on any
terminal, and print on a printer connected to the
terminal, a list, in chronological order, of all items
booked by a specific borrower. The display must
include at least the following information: borrower
name, address, telephone number, and unique identifier;
for each item, the title, call number, unique
identifier, booking date, and pickup location or
shipping date.

The system must have the capability to display on any
terminal, and print on a printer connected to the

terminal, a list of items, arranged alphabetically by
borrower name, which are scheduled to be picked up at a
specified location on any given day. The information
displayed must include at least the borrower name,
telephone number, and unique identifier; for each item,
the title, call number, unique identifier, date and
time of use, and pickup location.

The system must have the capability to display on any
terminal, and print on a printer connected to the
terminal, a list of items which are scheduled to be
shipped from a specified location on any given day.
The information displayed must include at least the
borrower name, telephone number, and unique identifier;
address of destination; and, for each item, the title,
call number, and unique identifier, date of use and any
special shipping instructions.

It must be possible for library staff to alter or
cancel any booking online.

It is desirable that the system be able to display a
list of items belonging to a specific branch library
which are not booked for a given date.

The system must have the capability to display on any
terminal, and print on a printer connected to the
terminal, a list of items due at a specified location
on any given day. Information displayed must include
at least the item title, call number and unique
identifier, borrower name and telephone number.

It must be possible for any _____ branch or library of
the ____ to book any item owned regardless of the
item's location.

The file updates associated with the Booking Function
must be done in real time.

Booked items must be circulated using the normal Charge
Function. All other functions, except the Hold
Function, which have to do with circulating items must
operate normally with booked items. It must not be
possible to place a hold on an item which must be
booked.

APPENDIX B / FUNCTIONAL SPECIFICATIONS

The system must automatically provide for a period of
time for cleaning and maintenance between bookings for
an item. It is desirable that it be possible to
specify different periods of time for different items.
It must be possible to modify the time period(s) easily
without programmer intervention.

It must be possible for library staff to determine
instantly, via terminal display, any bookings relating
to a specific item, including date and time of use,
shipping instructions, if any, and the name and unique
identifier of the borrower.

The system must be able to reassign the appropriate
status for any item not picked up on scheduled date.

The system must provide audible and visual signals,
easily distinguishable from normal transaction signals,
and the system must interrupt the booking transacion
when:

-- there is no item record for the item unique
   identifier entered;

-- there is no borrower record for the borrower
   unique identifier entered;

-- the item is already booked for the time
   specified;

-- the time specified for pickup or shipping does
   not allow for required maintenance time for the
   item;

-- the time specified for pickup or shipping is
   when the member library will be closed;

-- the borrower has a status of "delinquent;"

-- the item has a status of "lost," "missing,"
   "damaged," or "claims returned;"

-- on specified items (e.g., film projector), the
   borrower needs to successfully complete a
   proficiency test; needs to accept
   responsibility for the cost of the material by

125

signing a contract; needs to place a security
deposit. Once these tasks have been
successfully completed, the system may proceed.

The system must provide information in detail about
which of the above conditions caused the booking
transaction to be interrupted. The system must allow
authorized library staff to continue the booking
transaction after entering a password.

Interlibrary Loan (outside system)

The Circulation System will support the Library's role
in interlibrary lending activities by:

-- providing for charging/discharging an item
   which does not belong to a library of the
   system;

-- providing special loan period for issuing of
   _____ materials to other libraries;

-- providing additional overdue notice format for
   notifying a borrowing library of outstanding
   materials.

-- maintaining separate statistics for
   interlibrary loan usage.

-- statistics for interlibrary loan include:

     number of borrowing transactions;
     number of lending transactions;
     borrowing and lending statistics by name of
     other libraries and cooperative network.

-- the system must provide a copyright violation
   alert system which notifies an operator that
   the library has made the stipulated number of
   copies allowable by law.

Report Function

Each vendor must supply, as part of the proposal,
samples of all reports produced by the proposed system
and indicate the degree of flexibility available to _____

126

in developing cross-tabulated statistics and
additional reports.

The system must collect at least the statistics
necessary for the production of the reports specified
below. For each report it should be possible to have
the report automatically produced at specified
intervals or on demand.

It is desirable that it be possible to display on a
terminal the information specified for each report.

For each report specified below, the specification
gives the information required, the arrangement if
appropriate, the level of aggregation, and the time
period(s) to be covered. The highest level of
aggregation will be _____, so for each report the system
must be able to produce a separate report for _____ as a
whole, a separate report for each _____ branch, and for a
specified grouping of branches.

number of borrowers registered and cancelled - by branch
and collective total - monthly (M), and year-to-date
(YTD);

total number of borrowers itemized by category, age,
geographic code, sex - by branch and collective total -
M & YTD;

circulation statistics itemized by type of item,
material format, call number category, borrower
category, geographic code - by branch and collective
total - H (hourly), D (daily), M & YTD;

amounts of service charges owed, paid, and deleted - by
branch and collective total - M & YTD;

number of overdue notices sent, itemized by type of
notice - by branch and collective total - M & YTD;

number of fines deleted and amount, itemized by staff
password - by branch and collective total - M & YTD;

number of holds taken, satisfied, and cancelled - by
branch and collective total - M & YTD;

list of items in title order with more than the
specified number of holds - by branch - W (weekly);

list of items in title order on hold shelf not picked
up - by branch - W & YTD;

list of reserve book room items by course name and/or
faculty member (each group of items in title order);
[optional]

circulation statistics for reserve book room items (see
"c" above) - by branch and collective total - H, D, M &
YTD; [optional]

total number of cataloged volumes, gross number added
and number deleted, itemized by material format and
type and correlated with "h" above - by branch and
collective total - M & YTD;

total number of cataloged titles, gross number added
and number deleted itemized by material format and type
and correlated with "h" above - by branch and collective
total - M & YTD;

same reports as specified in "m" and "n" above for
uncataloged materials to extent permitted by level of
detail of temporary brief bibliographic record;

list of items in title order lost or reported lost for
more than specified time period - by branch and
collective total - W, M & YTD;

list of all last copy withdrawals arranged by title -
by branch and collective total - W, M & YTD;

number of items assigned to each branch library by
material format and type - by branch library and
collective total - M & YTD;

number of rotation books received in each branch
library by material format and type - branch library
and collective total - M & YTD;

number of items booked - by branch and collective total
- M & YTD;

list of delinquent borrowers unique identification
number and status of delinquent to include number of
books and/or list of books with password access
(supervisory) - M;

capability to draw comparative totals and/or
percentages from reports listed above for library
specified time periods;

list of fee and non-fee non-resident cards - by branch
and collective total - W, M, & YTD;

list of the names and locations of resident library for
non-resident - by branch and collective total - M &
YTD:

list of items on hold with no change in status for x
days - by branch and collective total - W & YTD;

number of items borrowed via intraloan - by branch and
collective total - M & YTD;

number of items loaned and borrowed via interlibrary
loan - by branch and collective total - M & YTD;

Inventory Function

Definition: a procedure by which a library verifies
the accuracy of the recorded status of each item in the
collection.

Library staff must be able to use the system to conduct
an inventory of a library, branch library, or part of a
branch library by entering the item unique identifier
either by scanning or keying. Each vendor must
describe in the proposal the inventory procedure
included in the proposed system. It is desirable that
the proposed procedure not require physically removing
the item from the shelf. The system must be able
to perform inventory and the normal circulation
functions concurrently during normal working hours.

The system must produce a report or reports for each
inventory project which lists:

        items on the shelf which have a status of

other than "on shelf;"

items not on the shelf which have a status of "on shelf;"

items which have not circulated in library specified period of time;

items with publication date prior to library specified date.

These items must be listed in call number order or author order as required. The item listing must include at least the item unique identifier, item call number, title, author, and status.

The system must automatically enter the date of the inventory into the record for each item inventoried.

The system should provide audible signals for items that are misshelved at the time found on the shelf.

Inquiry Function

Definition: the procedure by which one searches online files using a CRT terminal.

Inquiry requests must be entered on a keyboard, and inquiry request results must be displayed on a CRT terminal screen.

It must be possible to print whatever is displayed on a terminal screen on a printer connected to the terminal.

The system should employ string search key for inquiry rather than a derived search code key.

It should be possible to truncate some or all string searches.

It is desirable that it be possible to combine two or more search keys in one search using Boolean operators.

Access to files must be directly through the system and must not require library staff to check a list, file, or any other manual tool.

APPENDIX B / FUNCTIONAL SPECIFICATIONS

It must be possible to obtain a two level display, as a result of a successful inquiry in the bibliographic file. The first includes, but is not limited to, the following data elements: main entry, author, title, edition, publisher, date of publication, number of copies owned, number of holds, status of each copy, location of each copy, call number of each copy, item unique identifier for each copy, due date for each copy that is charged out. This first level display must not include MARC tags. The second level display includes all the above plus MARC tags.

It must be possible to obtain a display, as a result of a successful inquiry in the borrower file, which includes at least the following data elements: name, address, telephone number, borrower unique identifier, geographic code, category, status, where registered, total amount of fines/service charges owed, number of holds, number of claims returned, date registered, and local note. Additional displays must be available which show an itemized list of fines/service charges owed, and all other borrower data elements. Access to these displays must be password controlled.

Each vendor must describe in the proposal system response (i.e., output on CRT terminal) to an inquiry in the bibliographic file that (1) results in one hit; (2) results in more than one hit; (3) results in no hit.

Each vendor must describe in the proposal how many staff-terminal interactions are required (1) to obtain a display which shows status of copies in the branch library where the search is being done, and (2) to obtain a display which shows the status of copies in other branch libraries.

Each vendor must provide samples of screen formats for all inquiry displays in the proposal.

It must be possible to obtain a display, as a result of a successful inquiry in the item file, which includes at least the following data elements: main entry, title, edition, publisher, date of publication, call number, and all item data elements, including location.

131

APPENDIX B / FUNCTIONAL SPECIFICATIONS

Each vendor must describe in the proposal system response the levels of security via password protection; the possibility of restricting the number of functions on library specified terminals; the possibility of restriction on specified dial-a-ports.

It is desirable that the system include a set of prompts which can be used by any person using the inquiry function. Each vendor must describe in the proposal any such set of prompts included in the proposed system.

Message Function

In addition to routine messaging from the CPU console, the system must provide for inter-branch and system-wide messaging which will not interrupt on-going activities at the branch library. The general messages to all branches must be posted and available on request from the branch. An additional desirable feature would be an emergency interrupt that would display the holds that have been placed on materials that are sitting on the shelf of a branch and messages between libraries.

The message must _not_ interrupt an on-going function or display a message on a screen for an on-going function at the receiving terminals. The receiving terminals must indicate by means of a signal that a message has been received. In confirming a hold, the Library has the option to phone another library to ascertain whether the item is actually available. If it is, the item will be mailed to the patron or held at the library for later pickup by the patron or sent in delivery to the originating library.

An alert (one character, blinking preferred) must be displayed on the CRT screen, e.g., upper right-hand corner, in all functions to indicate one or more messages are waiting to be received by the terminal. After messages have been received, the alert character must cease to display until another message is sent to the terminal.

If no messages are received by closing time at a terminal with messages waiting, then a notice must be printed.

How many messages can be stored for any one branch?
How many messages can be stored system wide?

SUB-SYSTEM A

ACQUISITIONS

Selection List

Definition: a printed list with annotations
of new titles available for purchase that is
made available to the branches for selection.

The system must provide an efficient method
of compiling the selected titles for review
and then for purchase.

Common Data Base

The system must share the same title
bibliographic data base for both the
acquisition sub-system and the circulation
sub-system.

Method of Data Entry

The system must enter data through a computer
terminal in a direct and interactive manner,
using such prompting as is necessary to
maximize operator efficiency.

Fund Accounts

The system must be able to order multiple
copies and allocate them to multiple funds.
What are the limits for the system in terms
of the number of fund accounts and the
maximum size for an account number?

Discount Matrix

The system must store a discount matrix for a minumum of ten (10) jobbers/publishers. The discount matrix must store the appropriate discount rates based on a combination of type of publication (adult, juvenile, science or technical, speciality, etc.) and binding class (trade, paperback, paper, library, etc.). The discount matrix must be easily maintained by the library staff without vendor assistance.

Online Arithmetic Computations

The system must automatically perform all arithmetic operations and display the current account status pertaining to the fund and prevent overcharging the fund allocation with both visual and audio signals. There must be an override allowing an account to be overcharged.

Order Screen

The system must be capable of searching when an inquiry is made to ascertain if the bibliographic information is already in the data base:

> If not found: The operator enters the known bibliographic information along with the appropriate order information, e.g., jobber/publisher, number of copies ordered, list price, order type, prepayment required, status, etc.

> If data found: Data is to be displayed on the order form screen and additional copies may be ordered.

> Transferring data: Optionally, input may be from a vendor's online acquisition system.

Access to the Data

APPENDIX B / FUNCTIONAL SPECIFICATIONS

The system must restrict access to the
acquisition system to specific terminals and
password controls. Access to the status of
any item or title must be available from any
terminal.

Access to the acquisition system data shall
include:

-- Fund Account number including sub
   account
-- purchase order number
-- jobber or publisher name
-- jobber or publisher code
-- jobber or publisher invoice number

Purchase Orders

The system should be capable of transmitting
purchase orders (PO) without the need for a
printed copy through a book vendor's online
acquisitions system. The two systems would
need to interface so the in-house system
would receive the information from the book
vendor.

The system must be capable of entering a
group of books under one PO and entered as
i.e., "100 paperback titles."

Printing Purchase Orders

The system must be capable of printing
purchase orders (PO) on demand or on a
regular schedule. The operator may specify
the printing of:

-- all POs for a specific jobber or
   publisher
-- a specific PO number or a range of PO
   numbers
-- all POs

It is desirable that the system print orders
by order type (rush, normal) and by payment
type (bill, prepayment, standing

orders, etc.).

The system must issue a new PO when the publisher/jobber changes within a fund account.

The system must allow confirming type POs.

Standard Order Form

All POs will be printed on standard 3 X 5 order slips and 8 1/2 X 11 PO forms.

A pressure sensitive mailing label will be printed for each jobber

The system will assign unique PO numbers for all orders, either batch or online to the jobber.

Claiming Date

The system automatically calculates and stores a claiming date at the time the PO is entered. The claiming date is based on a combination of the date ordered and the type of material and the jobber/publisher from which the title is ordered. If possible, describe alternative claiming algorithms which may be used.

Vendor File

The system must provide a separate file containing jobber/publisher names and addresses. Some publishers have a separate address for sending of monies as opposed to orders which the system must maintain as well.

The system must provide, in addition to names and addresses, an indication of those publishers that must be ordered direct. The ISBN prefix may be stored and double checked at the time the ISBN is entered in the order entry screen.

The system must provide a list of
jobber/publishers with no activity for the
last 36 months. Upon operator instruction,
these may be purged from the system.

Online Status Changes

The system must provide a means to update
online the status and date of an order/title.

The status codes will include at least the
following:

B/O-L B/O-S	-	Back Ordered - Temporarily out of stock
B/O-N B/O-M	- -	Back Ordered - Not a stock title, supplied upon demand
WR B/O	-	"When Ready" title not yet available - back ordered
POL B/O	-	Publisher out of stock - back ordered
RES-L RES-S RES-N RES-M	-	Title has been received from publisher in next backorder shipment
PEND	-	Pending - Title in the process of being shipped and billed
PEND-WR -POL	-	Pending - Report only in the process of being reported on next shipment invoice
OP	-	Out of Print - Cancelled
AD	-	Order Direct - Cancelled
S	-	Subscription, order direct - Cancelled

137

PNS   - Publisher Not Supplied - Cancelled

TNS   - Title Not Supplied - Cancelled

PFR   - Publisher Failed to Respond -
             Cancelled

PC   - Publication cancelled

CF *CAN* - Cannot Find - Canceled due to
             cancellation date on this order

NOP "CAN" - Publisher reports not their
             publication - Cancelled due to
             cancellation date on this order

POS *CAN* - We and publisher out of stock -
             Cancelled

TOS *CAN* - Temporarily out of stock -
            Cancelled due to cancellation
            date on this order

Want List Report

The system must store Out of Print status for
an x month period. A monthly want list
report will be printed as an ordering aid.
An operator will delete upon command "Out of
Print" orders.

Claims Notice

The system shall prepare a claims notice to
be sent to the jobber/publisher for all items
on order longer than N days, N to be determined
by the library.

Order Cancellation Notice

The system must provide order cancelled
notices to be sent to the jobber/publisher
after N days, N to be determined by the
library. Funds encumbered must be returned
to allocation. A report must be prepared
listing all titles cancelled on a weekly

basis.

Receipt of Items

Receipt Screen

The system must provide a separate function to indicate receipt of items. A record is retrieved and the clerk verifies the order information. The operator then enters the quantity received, prices, information about damaged items and the back orders. The system automatically adds the date received.

Receiving Work Slip

After each title is entered as received a work slip must be printed with author, title, price and the number of copies ordered for each location.

Full Record

The system must indicate whether the system has received a full MARC record for the received title or only contains a brief record entered by the acquisitions clerk.

MARC Record Replacement

The system must enable a full MARC record to be overlaid on an existing brief acquisitions record, assuming appropriate verification of information, i.e., ISBN, LCCN, ISSN, author,title all match without the necessity of an operator deleting the brief acquisitions record. It is desirable that this system accept MARC records from magnetic tapes.

Accounting

Fund Adjustments

The system must facilitate adjustments

between funds, and credit and debit a
jobber/publisher.

Other Charges

Other jobber/publisher charges such as
shipping, insurance, and other charges will
be pro-rated among all the items on an
invoice. The value of the item price field
must be the list price less any discounts
plus a pro-rated share of the other charges
from the invoice.

Voucher Preparation

A report should be prepared for each
individual jobber of all ivoices between N
date and N date that have been approved for
payment.

Financial Audit Trail

The system must produce a listing on demand
of all financial transactions including fund
transfer, fund transactions, amount
allocated, amount encumbered, etc. either for
one account or for all accounts.

Vendor Performance Reports

Reports prepared on demand or on a regular
schedule, by jobber/publisher with more than
X dollars worth of orders must include:

Average number of days from date of order to
receipt of item.

Purchase Order Status Report indicating
status, encumbrance, dollars paid and
remaining balance for each jobber.

Calculate cost per volume for adult (fiction
and non-fiction) and juvenile (fiction and
non-fiction) works and produce a report at
the end of the fiscal year.

Monthly and YTD dollars paid and dollars encumbered, by fund and total.

Invoices by jobber that have been approved for payment.

Standing Orders

Standing orders must have all the features indicated above with the following additions:

The ability to enter a new claiming date for the next issue without printing a purchase order.

A report of all items that are N days past the claiming date.

Charging the cost to the appropriate account, keeping the record active, and not removing it to a historical file.

On demand, a list by branch by title of all standing orders on order for that branch. Expected cost must be included.

Provide a ship-to-address on the standing order PO when the item is to go directly to the branch.

The ability to enter a renewal date that will generate a report one month before the renewal date.

COM Tape Production

The system will, on demand, produce a computer tape formatted for COM production of a Subject Guide consisting of all subject terms used in the catalog with each subject term followed by the Dewey class numbers of all books to which that subject term has been assigned.

The system will, on demand, produce a computer tape formatted for COM production of a title-sequence listing consisting of title, author, date of publication, call number and accession number.

The system will, on demand, produce_a computer tape formatted for COM production of an author-sequence listing consisting of author, title, date of publication, call number and accession number.

SUB-SYSTEM B

ADMINISTRATION

General

The system must provide underpassword control and restricted access at specified terminals for basic personnel records, payroll, and accounting functions - including issuance of payroll and vendor checks - the minimum functions specified in this section. It is anticipated that the administrative sub-system proposed by the vendor will have additional capabilities not herein specified.

If this sub-system is not immediately available the successful vendor, upon signing of a contract with _____, must be willing to convert another program written for these functions into the lalnguage and data base manager utilized for the circulation system. This conversion must be accomplished within six months of contract signing at a cost clearly stated in the vendor's proposal, staff training provided, and have this sub-system fully debugged and operational by _____.

Under password control personnel, payroll, and account records and reports must be easily changed, rearranged and maintained by the library staff without vendor assistance, and must not require a high level of data processing expertise on the part of the library staff.

The system must enter data throgh a computer terminal in a direct and interactive manner, using such prompting as is necessary to maximize operator efficiency.

File Structure

Whether or not the data elements described below reside in the same file or in different files, the system must be designed so that the library office staff, under password control, can display and/or print out any personnel record and any payroll record in the administrative data base.

This sub-system must be thoroughly compatible with the acquisition sub-system and its fund accounts, purchase orders and their printing, accounting, receipt of items and accounting reports specifications. These sub-functions specifications must be fully integrated as part of the administrative sub-system.

The system must include safeguards which make it impossible for any person to destroy an entire file using a terminal. It is understood that the contents of an individual record may be altered using a terminal with proper password(s).

The records and their fields must be of sufficient length to accommodate the type and quantity of information required by administrative operations.

The system must have the capability to display on specified terminal(s) with proper password(s) all of the information in all of the files.

Personnel Record Data Elements

employee unique identifier [number]
full name with last name first
full address
telephone number
alternate telephone number
birthdate
social security number
job classification title (up to 30)
pay step level (up to 25)
base rate of pay - hourly, bi-weekly, annual
employment status:
     1)   administration
     2)   full-time
     3)   part-time
     4)   temporary
     5)   disability (with beginning date)
cost center (location of work site) - number
and name
scheduled hours per week
employee benefit and seniority dates
     1)   continuous service date - including
         longevity percentage rate
     2)   anniversary date - including step
         level
     3)   hire-in date
     4)   vacation benefit date - including
         annual accrual rate
     5)   personal time benefit date -
         including net accrual
     6)   seniority date
     7)   retirement date [credited service]
     8)   probation end date
     9)   evaluation due date
union bargaining unit
deductions (numbers) claimed (up to 5)
     1)   income tax
     2)   medical insurance
     3)   dental insurance
statutory deductions (up to 8)
other deductions (up to 25)
cumulate (add and subtract) for
administration, full-time and part-time
employees:
     1)   hours earned and used:
         i) vacation

        ii) personal time
   2) hours worked toward increases and notification [automatically printed out] to _____ 160 hours prior to increases or date due:
      i) pay steps (same as anniversary date
     ii) longevity
    iii) vacation
     iv) probation ending date
      v) evaluation due (same as anniversary date)

cumulate total hours worked by each employee (with separate cumulation of over-time hours).

leaves of absences - record beginning and ending date and cumulate hours used:
   1) personal
   2) bereavement
   3) educational
   4) jury duty
   5) court
   6) union educational
   7) union business
   8) military
   9) other

direct deposit

Payroll Data Elements

employee unique identifier [number]
full name with last name first
full address
social security number
job classification title (up to 30)
base rates - hourly and annnual
   1) wages
   2) longevity
   3) cost of living
   4) overtime (1.5 hourly wage rate) - hourly only
wage increases/changes
   1) pay step with anniversary date due
   2) negotiated percentage and/or dollar amount, with date due
   3) longevity, percentage and dollar

amount with date due
4) cost of living [March 1, June 1,
September 1, December 1]
employment status:
1) administration
2) full-time
3) part-time
4) temporary
5) disability
cost center - ID number and name
hours worked and gross wages (bi-weekly):
1) regular
2) vacation
3) personal time
4) holiday [annual list must be capable
of being added by staff without
vendor assistance]
5) overtime [at separate 1.5 hourly
rate]
6) leave of absence
7) total of numbers 1 through 6 above
longevity
1) hourly rate and annual amount

2) annual percentage
3) date increase due
quarterly cost of living (C.O.L.A.) amount
[March 1, June 1, September 1, December 1]
statutory deductions (up to 8)
1) federal income tax
2) state of _____ income tax
3) city of _____ income tax
4) social security (F.I.C.A.) tax -
employee
5) social security (F.I.C.A.) tax -
employer
other deductions (up to 25) with separate
employee and employer rates and costs where
applicable
1) retirement system
2) medical insurance
3) dental insurance
4) life and short-term disability
insurance
5) long term disability insurance
6) workman's compensation insurance

146

    7)   union dues
    8)   credit union
    9)   U.S. Savings Bonds
  10) United Way
  11) tax shelter (must handle up to 5
        different plans)

net pay (bi-weekly and annual)
union bargaining unit
direct deposit
    1)   name of bank and branch
    2)   full address
    3)   account number(s)

Bi-Weekly Payroll

This sub-system must be capable of printing bi-weekly payroll checks in format to be specified by _____ on printer used with the circulation system upon use of proper password(s) and restricted access at specified terminals and at CPU/printers.

Payroll and Personnel Reports

General

The system must collect at least the statistics necessary for the production of the reports specified below. For each report it should be possible to have the report produced automatically at specified intervals or on demand, whether latter is specified or not.

It is desirable that it be possible to display on a terminal for any part or all information specified for each report in addition to having it printed out.

For each report specified below the specifications give the formation required (See Personnel and Payroll data elements for required information sub-categories within an information category - e.g., hours and wages), the arrangement if appropriate, the

147

level of aggregation, and the time period(s) to be covered.

Other reports not specified must be capable of being produced from the data files by simple opeerator instructions which do not require vendor assistance.

Reports Required

Pay Stubs: hours and gross wages, longevity amount, quarterly cost of living amount, statutory deductions, other deductions, net pay, direct deposit, net hours available of vacation and of personal time - bi-weekly (BW) and year-to-date (YTD) totals each category and sub-category - BW;

Payroll Register: listing of each employee alphabetically with pay step changes, hours and gross wages (bi-weekly) longevity amount, quarterly cost of living amount, employee statutory deductions, employee other deductions, net pay, direct deposit BW & YTD totals each category and sub-category - BW;

Employee Earnings: separate listing of each employee with all payroll data elements - summary of each bi-weekly payroll register data in quarter with BW, quarterly (Q) and YTD totals for each category and sub-category - Q [March 31, June 30, September 30, December 31];

Cost Center: listing summary by each employment satus for each cost center of hours and gross wages, longevity amount, quarterly cost of living amount, employer deductions, net pay - monthly (M), current quarter & YTD totals each category and sub-category - M & Q [March 31, June 30, September 30, December 31];

W-2 Forms: completed W-2 forms with annual total gross pay and each employee statutory deduction - annual (A) within first five (5) working days of January each year;

Retirement Report: listing of each employee
alphabetically with employee and employer
separate costs and total of both - M & YTD
totals for each employee and for all
employees - M & annual (A);

Insurance Costs: listing of each employee
alphabetically of employer cost of retirement
system and each insurance (medical, dental,
life and short term disability, long term
disability, workman's compensation) - M & YTD
totals of each sub-category for all employees
- M & Q;

Hours Scheduled/Worked: listing summary by
each employment status subdivided by each job
classification for each cost center of number
of employees, total number bi-weekly hours
scheduled and bi-weekly hours (including each
sub-category), difference (plus or minus
between scheduled and total hours) - M & YTD
totals each category and sub-category by cost
center, grouping of cost centers, and _____
cumulative totals - M & Q;

Union Seniority: listing of each employee
within each job classification title by
seniority date with separate listings for each
union bargaining unit - on demand;

Wages Projection: listing of each employee
alphabetically by each employment status
(omitting Temporary) with these calculations
in columns:

    1) start of year base (current annual
        rate of pay)
    2) pay step increase amount in current
        year
    3) year's annual wages (#1 & 2
        together)
    4) longevity amount in current year
    5) cost of living amount in current
        year

6) gross current annual wages (#3, 4, 5 together)
7) end of year base (#1 and 2 _annualized_ together)
8) negotiated pay increase, if any
9) 1% of #7, if requested
10) pay step increase amount in next year base (# 7 & 8 together)
11) pay step increase amount in next year
12) next year annual wage (#10 & 11 together)
13) longevity amount in next year
14) cost of living amount in next year
15) gross next annual wages (#12, 13, 14 together);

each column must be totaled for each employment status sub-category and totaled for all employees - on demand;

"Fringes" Projection: list of each employee alphabetically for all employment status sub-category with_employer_ costs of social security and each other deduction - total by each employee of social security and all other deductions sub-categories together; total for all employees of social security and each other deduction sub-category - on demand;

Staff Directory: one listing of each employee alphabetically for all employment status sub-categories - arranged by home telephone (with area code ___ omitted), employee name, full address, location (name of cost center, with specified ID series "translated" and printed as Headquaerters), continuous service date - Q & on demand.

Accounting

The system must be capable of maintaining all account information by separate calendar year for three years by fund accounts and sub-accounts, cost centers, and specified groupings of each with budgeted amounts and monthly and year-to-date encumbered and expenditure totals or by any other arrangement specified by the library. Upon operator instruction data may be purged from the system, including the oldest year's data in its entirety.

The accounts and records must be maintained on daily, monthly and year-to-date basis.

The system must provide minimally up to one hundred (100) fund accounts and sub-accounts, up to forty (40) cost centers, and specified groupings of each with data entered simultaneously in each.

The system must provide comparative totals and percentages for library specified time periods.

The system must provide a separate file containing up to two hundred fifty (250) vendor names, addresses, and telephone numbers.

Accounts Receivable

Maintain record of all money received and all money deposited in bank accounts from all sources (up to 25 categories and 200 sub-categories) by individual branch library, where appropriate, and _____ collectively. Records must include date received, amount, source, date of deposit, bank account number(s).

Accounts Payable

Maintain numerical, open purchase order file by PO number with all information contained on the purchase order.

Record monies encumbered by fund account and sub-account, cost center, and specified groupings of each. When payment is made to vendors the system must automatically remove the amount encumbered - full or partial - and record in actual expenditures amount by fund account and sub-account, cost center, and specified groupings of each.

This sub-system must be capable of printing on demand vendor payment checks in format to be specified by _____ on printer used with circulation system upon use of proper password(s) and restricted access at specified terminals and at CPU/printer.

Maintain numerical vendor check issued file by check number and record payment by fund account and sub-account, cost center, and specified groupings of each.

Maintain alphabetical closed purchase order file by vendor name and by item purchased with information contained on the purchase order.

Account Reports

For reports specified below the specifications give the information required, the arrangement if appropriate, the level of aggregation, and the time period(s) to be covered.

Other reports not specified must be capable of being produced from the data files by simple operator instructions which do not require vendor assistance.

Reports Required

_____ budget: budgeted amount, encumbered funds, actual expenditures totalled together), comparison to previous year by fund account and sub-account and specified groupings - monthly (M) and year-to-date (YTD) totals - M, quarterly (Q) and on demand;

Cost Center budget: same information and

totals as in _____ budget report - Q and on demand;

General Ledger: same information and totals in both _____ budget and Cost Center budget reports with numerical listing of each check paid, vendor name, and amount - M and on demand;

Monthly Check Register: numerical listing by each check number and amount - continual monthly net balance (total of all checks in month subtracted from specified bank account balance) - M;

Monthly Receipts: money received by source - monthly and year-to-date totals - M and on demand.

Word Processor

_____ requires a shared-logic word processor with CRT display screen and diskette storage.

Provide detailed description of equipment proposed and of any alternate equipment which is compatible with vendor's CPU.

Describe anti-power loss feature.

SUB-SYSTEM C

INTERFACES

Future growth of the use of automated circulation systems locally, within the state and regionally, will require interfaces between like and unlike types of systems. _____'s librarians require an unequivocal commitment from vendors that they will provide technical assistance toward accomplishing these interfaces and that nothing in their sales or lease contract prohibits _____ from offering access to its data to users of other systems.

Futhermore, _____ requires a statement from each vendor that acknowledges commitment to a willingness to cooperate toward achieving interconnections with other systems of its type, with systems of other vendors, and with bibliographic data networks and information utilities in existence or under development.

SUB-SYSTEMS, FUTURE

Specifically, the system should be capable of being expanded to include:

serials control system (no functional specifications developed to date);

Online Catalog System

The vendor is requested to outline plans for adding these or any other planned subsystems to the system it proposes to provide in response to requirements stated elsewhere in this document, and to estimate numbers of additional online transactions and terminals that these future subsystems would require during peak hours.

The vendor is asked to present evidence of its state-of-development of each such subsystem according to the following:

how many installations are using the subsystem?

has field testing of the subsystem been completed?

is the subsystem currently undergoing field testing?

what further development and testing of the subsystem is planned and what are the schedules for these activities?

Public Online Catalog

The system proposed must have the growth potential to function as an online catalog.

This additional utilization of the data base must be realized simply by upgrades to the central site hardware.

Multiple screen formats designed for use by patrons and, hence, excluding all MARC II tags and indicators, are required for accessing the biblioraphic data base by various indices, e.g., author, title, author/title, subject. The user must be able to enter full or partial (except author/title) strings. Access method must facilitate browsing. Vendor will describe how such access will be supported.

The system proposed will employ "prompts" to assist the untrained user. Such prompts should be available at any point in the search. If the search is excessively complex, the system should direct the user to the librarian.

APPENDIX C

Examples of Technical Specifications

Equipment Specifications

All equipment proposed must be new, i.e., previously unused at any other site.

For all equipment proposed, each vendor must specify the original manufacturer's name and model number on the forms provided in this RFP and attach a copy of the equipment specifications. In addition, for all individual components each vendor must specify the vendor's suggested Mean Time Between Failures (MTBF) and Mean Time to Repair (MTTR). Each vendor must provide additional items of information about specific components as specified in the following sections.

Each proposal must include a detailed system diagram illustrating the complete system configuration. This diagram must include the recommended telecommunications network with lines and line speeds, telecommunications equipment (e.g., modems, multiplexors, etc.), terminals, printers, and all CPU site equipment including high speed printers and console.

The equipment proposed must be able to function according to the specifications outlined in this RFP for a growth period for _____ of five (5) years from date of installation of the system. See Appendices A & B for estimated total growth. It is understood that if terminals are added beyond the number specified in this RFP, it may be necessary to add main memory.

The system must be supported by a CPU or CPUs totally dedicated to the online integrated library system. The system must be able to

157

handle up to fifty (50) interactive terminals without changing the CPU or adding main memory. In addition to the information required for all equipment, each vendor must provide the following items of information for each CPU proposed:

a. capacity of main memory (number of K bytes)

b. access and cycle time

c. date of first installation as configured

d. total number of configurations this size installed to date

e. maximum number of terminals and disks the CPU will support as configured without the loss of response time

f. the capability of each system of multipoint communication circuits (polling environment)

At least one magnetic tape drive for file backup and initial file loading is required. Tape drive(s) must be nine-track, at least 1600 bpi, at least 45 ips, must use 2400 ft. capacity reels, and must have audible and visual failure indicators. Each vendor is requested to supply price information for a tape drive which is dual density, switchable from 800 bpi to 1600 bpi, in addition to price information for the tape drive(s) proposed.

The proposed system must include sufficient disk capacity to hold all files and indices, including a five-year growth period. The disk configuration must provide for backup procedures. Replaceable and interchangeble disk packs are required. Disk facilities may be partially fixed and partially moveable.

APPENDIX C / TECHNICAL SPECIFICATIONS

In addition to the information required for
all equipment, each vendor must provide the
following items of information for each disk
drive proposed:

    a. capacity (in megabytes) of proposed
       disk storage

    b. formula used to estimate disk space

    c. average access time, including
       latency; rotational delay

    d. data transfer rates, in
       kilobytes/seconds

One high-speed line printer to be located at
the CPU site is required. In addition to
the information required for all equipment,
each vendor must provide the following items
of information:

    a. type of reproduction if not impact

    b. number of high speed printers that
       can be accommodated with proposed
       CPU

    c. serial or parallel interface

    d. type of paper

One console keyboard and logging device to be
located at the CPU site is required.

All terminals proposed, except for support or
portable equipment discussed below, must be
interactive CRT's capable of handling full
ASCII character sets. All terminals proposed
must have parallel printer interfaces and
audio prompts. In addition to the
information required for all equipment, each
vendor must provide the following items of
information for each terminal proposed:

    a. baud rate(s) - minimum and maximum

b. is baud rate switchable?

c. full or half duplex?

d. include sample keyboard layout

e. is keyboard separable from main chassis?

f. number of characters/line and number of lines/screen

g. number of pages to screen

h. forward and backward scrolling

i. size of CRT screen (diagonally in inches)

j. size of characters

k. color of screen and characters

l. size of terminal buffer

It is desirable that the proposed system have the capability to utilize any of the various types of optical input devices currently available, such as OCR, bar code, laser scanner, etc. Each vendor must specify what types can be used with the proposed system and what type is recommended and why. Whatever type is recommended must correctly read the item unique identifier on the first attempt by a trained operator ninety percent (90%) of the time. In addition to the information required for all equipment, each vendor must provide the following items of information for each optical input device proposed:

a. character capacity

b. type and number of fonts read

    c. operator constraints:

        1) scanning speed range

        2) depth of field

        3) pen tilt limitations, if
            applicable

    d. data input/output rates

    e. type of interface

    f. type of device (OCR, bar code, etc.)
        (please specify all options
        available)

The proposed system must include low level
slave printers to be used in connection with
CRT terminals. These printers will be
connected to the CRT terminals via a printer
port on the CRT terminal and will be used to
print date due charge slips, routing slips,
receipts, borrower account records, and upon
request by the operator, whatever is
displayed on the CRT terminal screen at the
time of the request. The type of
reproduction must not produce much noise,
since these printers will be located in
public areas. It is suggested that the
printers proposed be similar in size,
characteristics, and cost to the Perkin Elmer
Pussycat printer. It is desirable, in a
branch library with more than one CRT
terminal but only one printer, that it be
possible to send data to the printer from any
one of the CRT terminals. In addition to the
information required for all equipment, each
vendor must provide the following items of
information for each printer proposed:

    a. speed

    b. type of reproduction if not impact

    c. size and type of buffered imput

    d.   serial or parallel interface?

    e.   number of slave printers that can be accommodated with proposed CPU

    f.   type of paper

    g.   any special features, such as forms control, printing in both directions, etc.

    h.   include sample of output from printer proposed

Operating Software

The vendor must identify all bundled and unbundled software and limit discussion of software to two packages.

Each vendor must provide in the proposal the following information about the operations software:

    a.   programming language of operating system

    b.   date of first release

    c.   number of releases since first release

    d.   do all compilers, tasks and routine and other systems programs run under control of this operating system? List any stand alone programs and specify their main control functions.

    e.   what is the name of the DBMS?

It is required that the vendor supply the latest release of the operating system within nine (9) months of its release and make appropriate modifications in the applications software.

APPENDIX C / TECHNICAL SPECIFICATIONS

Each vendor must specify the language in
which the teleprocessing module is written,
as well as the following:

    a. analog or digital transmission

    b. serial or parallel transmission

    c. asynchronous or synchronous
       transmission

Applications Software

The software and application programs must be
able to perform the functions specified under
the Functional Specifications, as well as the
necessary maintenance functions required by
the data bases. In addition, the vendor must
specify that the system has software
utilities or application programs which will
be able to control the following functions:

    a. unload and reload data bases

    b. provide backup procedures for data
       bases

    c. restoration of data bases after
       system failure

The vendor must also specify the
upgradability and transportability of the
software for future expansion.

Each vendor must agree to supply software
with license to _____ for its perpetual use
without necessity for additional royalty,
copyright, or other service fee. _____ shall
agree not to reproduce this software in any
form without the express written agreement of
the vendor.

Each vendor must specify in the proposal the
language(s) under which the applications
software is written and whether or not the

equipment manufacturer supplies a compiler
or assembler for the language(s) utilized.
Each vendor must also state whether or not a
read-only memory interpreter is furnished if
the language is interpretive.

_____ must have the option of implementing
additional applications software on the
system; however, the vendor will be required
to offer maintenance only on all vendor-
supplied software.

The applications software must be written to
employ terminal screen paging techniques,
with a back page capability, to permit
effective system training and eliminate the
need to re-enter commands because of screen
data "lost" due to scrolling.

The applications software must be written to
handle full MARC II records and to accept any
of the MARC II fields as search indices. The
number of indices allowed must not be less
than 25 and is to be specified by _____ prior
to the initial bibliographic file load. _____
must have the option to alter or respecify
the number of indices and reload the
bibliographic file without modification to
the vendor's software.

The applications software must be written to
employ priority task execution in a
parameter-driven mode for no less than ten
(10) priority elements, with charge/discharge
functions having highest priority.

The vendor must permit _____ access to the
applications software by use of a special
access password.

The vendor must furnish to _____, without
charge, any subsequent software releases of
this application.

The vendor must agree to place all
applications software documentation in

escrow, granting _____ access without restriction in the event the vendor should go into receivership or for any reason terminate business.

Each vendor must provide in the proposal complete descriptions of all files maintained by the applications software, record structures of all files, and details of all algorithms which access records in all files. The descriptions must make clear which files are accessed by hashing or keys and which are accessed through indexes.

Data Security and Recovery

The system must provide security to prevent accidental or unauthorized modification of records.

The system must provide two pyramid structures of authorization which are independent of each. The terminal identification pyramid is to have two levels:

   a. the highest level must have access to all aspects of the system, both equipment and software, including the ability to alter the authorization of these terminals

   b. the second level must permit circulation function overides and alteration of patron, bibliographic and item records

The operator identification pyramid is to have four levels:

   a. the highest level must permit access to all levels of the applications software, including the ability to alter the authorization level of all other operator identification codes

   b. the second level must permit

       alteration of patron, bibliographic,
       and item records and overrides of
       circulation functions

c. the third level must permit
   overrides of circulation functions

d. the fourth level must permit read
   access only to bibliographic and
   item records.

The system must have the ability to provide a
full recovery from any type of system
failure. The system must be able to
completely restore the day's data base after
any problem by using a transaction log and
backup copy of the data base or any other
nonmanual method proposed by vendors. It is
required that data security provisions
include daily backup of the disk files.

Each vendor must describe in the proposal the
operational backup procedures and the normal
and emergency recovery procedures including
the backup and recovery time (in minutes) as
follows:

	Time (in minutes)	
	Backup	Recovery
per 10,000 titles		
per 10,000 items		
per 10,000 borrowers		
per 10,000 outstanding circulation transactions		

Provisions for Downtime

It is required that the proposed system
include some provision for continuing at
least charge and discharge transactions when
the system is down. Such provision must not

166

require any manual logging of transactions
for keying at a later time and must not
involve the use of cassette devices for
logging transaction data. If such provision
involves collection of transaction data by
means of a solid state portable terminal, the
system must provide for quick and efficient
input of this data once the system is up.
Each vendor must provide detailed description
of these procedures, including time to input
a given number of transactions.

Engineering Standards

Where the output of an instrument is in
digital form, it must conform to EIA or
E.E.E.E. standards.

Instrument wiring must terminate at the
remote processor housing via multipin locking
connectors. Each pin must be labeled to
conform with schematics and interconnection
block diagrams and/or "from/to" connection
listings which must be included in
documentation supplied to _____. The vendor
must supply the mating connector.

All signal leads from instruments to
processor must be shielded. Shields must not
be used as a current carrying conductor.

All equipment and housings must be bonded to
one another via grounding straps, using good
engineering practice.

Equipment housing grounds, shielding grounds
and signal grounds, must be handled
separately. All signal grounds, including
those of instrumentation, must be brought to
one central point and there be grounded to
the equipment frame. Ground loops are to be
avoided.

Primary power circuits and circuits carrying
switching type currents must be dressed away
from sensitive, low current circuits.

167

Each instrument must be separately fused, and the fuses must be easily accessible without the use of tools. Fuse sizes must be clearly marked and must be easily replaceable without electrical hazard to a maintenance person.

All circuit interrupting components, relays, motors, circuit breakers, buzzers, choppers, and devices of similar nature must be equipped with transient supporters.

Signal conditions shall be physically independent to a channel to facilitate troubleshooting and replacement without disturbing the operations of other instruments.

Adjustment controls for calibration shall be clearly identified. Vendor shall make available any special tools required for adjustments. Controls shall be provided with a cloaking device or be mounted in a suitable enclosure to prevent accidental operation.

Where equipment is connected via common carrier data channels, EIA RS 232/C standard connectors shall be employed.

Label Specifications

Each vendor must specify in the proposal prices for machine coded labels in the following amounts:

   a. 500,000 label pairs with item
       unique identifiers

   b. 250,000 single labels with item
       unique identifiers

   c. 90,000 single labels with borrower
       unique identifiers

The machine coding may be either OCR or bar code; if it is bar code, there must be an eye-readable number on the label.

Label paper color must be white. Reflectance must be 70% or higher, gloss must not exceed 60% and opacity, including the backing, must be at least 85%

The labels must be water resistant and all labels must have a pressure sensitive adhesive backing.

If the labels are computer-generated, the surface should have a laminated coating to protect the carbon ink. The vendor must guarantee that whatever method is employed to produce the printed labels, the ink will not smear in normal usage and the labels will not require application of any additional spray coating or tape to protect the surface after application on borrower cards or library materials.

Each vendor must also specify a per label price in the proposal guaranteed for one year following acceptance of the proposal.

 Label Code Specifications

Each vendor must state in the proposal the number of characters each borrower unique identifier and item unique identifier requires and report the ultimate capacity in terms of number of borrowers and items the code will accommodate without additional characters. Borrower and item labels must be randomly assigned throughout _____.

The system must automatically check, through the use of a check digit, that both the borrower unique identifier and the item identifier have been accurately entered. The system must provide audible and visual signals that are easily distinguishable from the normal transaction signal if data entry is incomplete or incorrect. The vendor must specify in the proposal the formula used to generate the check digit.

The system must automatically prevent the interchange of a borrower unique identifier with an item unique identifier in all functions.

Telecommunications Network

Each vendor must include in the proposal a recommended telecommunications network design which specifies communications equipment and line configuration. It is desirable that the vendor include a discussion of recent trends and options in telecommunication, such as telecable. To what degree has the vendor experienced this? Specify what the vendor can supply. Justify the telecommunications network design on basis of present and future costs and service requirements.

For all equipment proposed as part of the telecommunications network, the vendor must provide the same information required for all other equipment. List alternative equipment that has been tested and found to be useable with the telecommunications network project, including manufacturer, model number and price.

The final choice of the telcommunications network will be made with the advice of the vendor, but final responsibility will rest with _____.

What are the credentials and experience of vendor's data communication engineer or specific staff expertise in this area?

Maintenance

The contracted periods of maintenance shall be 8:00 a.m. through 5:00 p.m. Monday through Friday (all times are Eastern time). On-call maintenance at times outside the contracted periods of maintenance must be available on a

per-hour charge basis. Each vendor must
specify in the proposal the itemized price of
on-call maintenance. Each vendor is
requested to specify in the proposal the
price for extended contracted maintenance
coverage for (1) the periods of 5:00 p.m.
through midnight Monday through Friday and
8:00 a.m. through 5:00 p.m. Saturday and
Sunday; and (2) the period of 8:00 a.m.
through 5:00 p.m. Saturday.

In the event of an equipment problem, it is
required that, during the contracted periods
of maintenance, a vendor maintenance
representative must be on-site within four
(4) hours of notification by an authorized
_____ representative that a problem exists.

The vendor should, as a feature of the
system, include a dial-up port so that vendor
personnel can provide software maintenance on
a remote or dial-up basis. In the event of a
software problem, it is required that, during
the contracted periods of maintenance, a
vendor maintenance representative must be
"on-site" ether in person or via the dial-up
port within two (2) hours of notification by
an authorized _____ representative that a
problem exists.

Each vendor must specify in the proposal for
each piece of equipment proposed the mean
time to repair and the number of hours it
requires per month for preventive maintenance
and the frequency and duration of such
preventive maintenance.

Each vendor must specify in the proposal a
designated point(s) of contact for
notification of equipment and/or software
problems.

Does _____ have the option to establish a
separate maintenance contract with third party
hardware manufacturers?

171

APPENDIX C / TECHNICAL SPECIFICATIONS

Delivery and Installation

Each vendor must include a Project Schedule in the proposal.

The events on this schedule should be organized in terms of the number of days from the date of issuance, from _____, of written notice to proceed. The schedule must show at least the following events: starting date; required facility readiness date (i.e., date the CPU site must be ready for equipment installation); pre-delivery test, equipment delivery; equipment installation; software installation; data base loading; conversion; staff training; acceptance testing; system operational.

All equipment, including terminals, must be delivered and installed within one hundred and eighty (180) days of the starting date.

Site preparation will be the responsibility of _____. For that reason, each vendor must provide a complete description of the electrical, air conditioning, humidity, and space requirements for the proposed system in the proposal for the CPU site. Indication should be given whether computer flooring is required, desirable, or unnecessary.

The vendor shall assume all costs of installation for the equipment required for the system, exclusive of site preparation, which shall be the responsibility of _____.
Costs for installation by the vendor or vendor's subcontractor shall be separately stated in the proposal to become part of the total cost for the system.

Miscellaneous Supplies

The vendor will be expected to supply, as part of the system, a one-year stock of supplies. This stock of supplies should include, but is not limited to, such items as

disk packs, magnetic tape, tape reels,
computer paper, notice and bill stock,
printer ribbons, printer paper (for both
types of printers).

Transaction Response Time

The system must give the highest priority to
the Charge Function. The system must
maintain the response times shown in the
following table for all transactions.
Response time is defined as that period of
time that begins when the "send" or "carriage
return" key is pressed and ends when the
first usable information begins being
displayed on the terminal screen as a result
of the command that was transmitted.

Function	Required response time (in seconds)	
	average	peak load times
charge, discharge, renewal	less than 2	2
inquiry	4	10
entering bibliographic, item, or borrower data via keyboard	less than 20	20
all other transactions	less than 2	3

See Appendix A for information on peak load
times.

System Reliability Acceptance Test

Once the equipment has been delivered,
installed, and connected to the power lines
and telephone lines supplied by the library,
the vendor shall certify in writing that the
system is operational and ready for use. In
addition, the vendor will have loaded the

_____'s bibliographic data base and branch locator file and successfully demonstrated that the system can accommodate the conversion of the _____ collections (entry of all necessary data, e.g., unique item number, owning library location, etc.) as well as start to build the patron data base.

All other equipment, e.g., modems, terminals, printers, etc., shall be installed and shown to be in good operating condition.

At this point the System Reliability Acceptance Test may begin. The system must operate at an average level of effectiveness of ninety-eight percent (98%) or more for a period of sixty (60) consecutive library work days, not calendar days, to meet the _____ standard of performance. Should the level of effectiveness not be met at any time during the test, average system downtime will have exceeded two percent (2%) for a 60 day period, and the System Reliability Acceptance Test will begin anew. The vendor will have a total of five (5) calendar months to successfully complete the test. The Library's scheduled hours of system availability will be used as the basis for computation of the average effectiveness level.

A Systems Reliability Acceptance Test procedure shall be jointly negotiated between the successful vendor and the Library. The Library shall insist on a formal reporting relationship through the use of system downtime logs, System Failure Report forms, and other aids as may be necessary.

The vendor shall make all reasonable adjustments and modifications of the system at its own cost and expense so that it will successfully perform in accordance with the System Reliability Acceptance Test within the prescribed five (5) month period. If unable to do so, then the Library has the option of

requiring that the vendor replace the
affected part(s) of the installed equipment
and then begin the System Reliability
Acceptance Test anew or to cancel the
contract and to seek damages from the vendor.

Functional Performance Acceptance Test

The purpose of the Functional Performance
Acceptance Test is to verify that the
software delivered actually performs those
functions the vendor agreed to provide in the
written proposal to _____ Request for Proposal
and contracted for by _____.

The Functional Performance Acceptance Test
shall commence after the successful
completion of the Systems and Reliability
Acceptance Test, and shall use _____
data files then in the system. Vendor
representatives are expected to observe and
assist in conducting the test.

Each function or procedure listed in the
contract between the vendor and _____ will each
be separately used and reviewed to ensure
that each function is provided and is
properly and accurately executed by the
computer system. Examples of functions to be
reviewed include, but are not limited to,
charge and discharge of items under a variety
of conditions; borrower and item inquiry,
subject inquiry, and telephone renewal; placing
a hold; and preparation of the required
management reports and notices.

Software shall not be accepted by _____ until
all of the required functions perform in a
satisfactory manner as documented in the
Functional Performance Acceptance Test.

Full-Load Response Time Acceptance Test

The Full-Load Response Time Acceptance Test
is intended to demonstrate that the system is
capable of meeting the response time criteria

175

at user terminals under full-load conditions.

Full-load shall mean a total of twenty-three (23) terminals attached to the computer. Twenty (20) terminals operating as circulation terminals will perform twenty (20) checkout and checkin transactions per minue per terminal. This terminal shall also be operating as inquiry terminal and a minimum of three (3) inquiries per minute per terminal of the borrower bibliographic, or item data base shall be made from each terminal. The terminal which will function as data entry terminal will enter title and item information or patron registration information at a rate of ten (10) items per hour per terminal. Ten (10) minutes after the start of the Full-Load Response Time Acceptance Test Data from a portable terminal (at least 150 circulation transactions) via the dial-in port shall be accepted and processed by the computer.

The Full-Load Response Time Acceptance Test shall commence after the successful completion of the prior two acceptance tests and at a time to be mutually arranged between _____ and the selected vendor. The duration of this final acceptance test shall be one (1) hour. _____ will provide terminal operators and data recorders for each terminal. At the end of the test all records and logs will be collected and the average response times for each category shall be computed by _____ personnel. The average response times shall be the total of all of the transaction times divided by the total number of all the transactions in that category at online terminals.

The Full-Load Response Time Acceptance Test shall be successfully met when the average response time for each response time category is within the response time standards as specified in Section

176

The total system shall not be accepted by _____ until the Full-Load Response Time Acceptance Test has been successfully conducted.

Repeated Performance of Acceptance Tests

If either the Functional Performance Acceptance Test or the Full-Load Response Time Acceptance Test shall not be successful, the vendor shall be expected to make whatever adjustments, modifications, or enlargements to the equipment or software as it deems necessary or desirable to obtain a successful acceptance test. Time spent and equipment installed to make modifications to effect a successful acceptance test shall be at the expense of the vendor and shall in no way be billed to _____. After adjustments and modifications, if any, the vendor shall notify _____ in writing that it desires to retry the previously unsuccessful acceptance test. The acceptance test(s) shall then be performed again as set forth in the procedures above.

The inability of the system to successfully complete any or all acceptance tests as described herein within five hundred forty-eight (548) consecutive calendar days of the date of issuance by _____ of written notice to begin work may be considered a contract default by the vendor and _____ shall not pay last installment due.

At the end of the time period if conditions are not met, _____ has the option of having the equipment removed, replaced, or at the option to cancel the contract. If the equipment is replaced, all acceptance tests shall begin anew.

The contractor shall certify in writing to the library when the equipment has met the Acceptance Tests and is ready for production use.

APPENDIX D

Examples of Miscellaneous Specifications

Miscellaneous

The system must not affect, or be affected by, the operation of book detection systems.

The system must be able to sort by Dewey Decimal call number, Library of Congress call number, ISBN, ISSN, as well as alphabetically by author or title.

It is desirable that the system have the capability to communicate with other installations of the same vendor for purposes of facilitating inter-library loan.

The proposed system must provide a transaction system to circulate items off-site with a portable device. Each vendor must describe in the proposal this provision.

File Design

The file structure must be integrated with a suitable data base management system.

Whether or not the data elements described below reside in the same file or in different files, the system must be designed so that each _____ branch can display any bibliographic record and any item record in the circulation data base.

It is required that the files be structured so that it is necessary to have only one bibliographic record for each edition of a title to which each _____ branch may attach one or more item records. Each vendor must describe how the proposed system meets this specification.

The system must include safeguards which make it impossible for any person to destroy an entire file using a terminal. It is understood that the contents

179

of an individual record may be altered using a terminal with proper password(s).

The records and their fields must be of sufficient length to accommodate the type and quantity of information required by system operations. All fixed and variable fields must be specified.

The system must have the capability to display on a terminal all of the information in all of the files.

Borrower File

The borrower file must be structured so that once a borrower has registered at one branch of _____, s/he can use any _____ library without having to re-register or receive another unique identifier.

Borrower records will be entered via keyboard and in machine readable form.

For new borrowers, the system must match the incoming records against existing borrower records, print out any duplicate records, and add records for which there are no duplicates.

It must be possible for authorized library staff to display, edit and update any borrower record.

Data Elements

Bibliographic data elements, full bibliographic record: the system must accommodate all variable length fields that are defined in the MARC II formats, except the linking entry fields in the serials format which are optional. It is estimated that the average size of these bibliographic records is 600 characters.

Bibliographic data elements, permanent brief bibliographic record:

    a. main entry
    b. author - full or partial
    c. title - full or partial
    d. publisher
    e. date of publication

    f.   added entries
    g.   subject headings
    h.   call number
    i.   ISBN or ISSN number
    j.   LC card number
    k.   format of materials

Bibliographic data elements, temporary brief bibliographic record:

    a.   author
    b.   title
    c.   item unique identifer
    d.   local note
    e.   ISBN number

Item record data elements:

    a.   item unique identifier
    b.   volume, issue, and/or copy designation
    c.   material type (up to 15)
    d.   material format (up to 10)
    e.   status (must be dual level, up to 10)
    f.   local call number
    g.   name of owning library
    h.   permanent location (i.e., branch)
    i.   temporary location
    j.   date of last circulation
    k.   number of circulations since entered system
    l.   local note
    m.   date of most recent inventory

Borrower record data elements:

    a.   borrower unique identifier
    b.   full name
    c.   full address
    d.   alternate address
    e.   telephone number
    f.   alternate telephone number
    g.   birthdate
    h.   social security number
    i.   sex
    j.   name of parent or guardian of minors
    k.   telephone number of parent or guardian of minors

l. geographic code
m. statistical category A (up to 6)
n. statistical category B (up to 6)
o. status (eligible or delinquent)
p. library of ____ area link, i.e., where registered
q. date registered
r. date of last transaction
s. number of holds
t. number of "claims returned" and "reported lost" used
u. number of items charged out currently
v. total amount of fines/service charges owed currently
w. local note

File Access

The system must have the capability to use the following fields or data elements as access points in the relevant file:

Full bibliographic record:

a. main entry, author (full or partial), added entry, subject heading
b. title
c. call number
d. Library or Congress card number
e. ISBN or ISSN number

Permanent brief bibliographic record:

a. main entry, author (partial or full), added entry, subject heading
b. title
c. call number
d. ISBN or ISSN number

Temporary brief bibliographic record:

a. item unique identifier
b. title

APPENDIX D / MISCELLANEOUS SPECIFICATIONS

Item record:

    a. item unique identifier

Borrower records:

    a. borrower unique identifier
    b. name
    c. name/address key (desired, not required)
    d. social security number

Authority Control

The system must provide authority files for personal and corporate names, series, and subject headings with appropriate cross references for each.

The system must accept LC distributed name and subject authority data as well as authority file input through a system terminal.

Each heading in the authority file must be linked to each occurence of that heading in the bibliographic file so that all occurrences of a heading can be modified with a single transaction.

As bibliographic records are being input or modified, the system will immediately alert the operator when a term not in the authority file is entered and provide a listing of related entries, including cross references where applicable.

The authority system must maintain "see" and "see also" references.

The authority file must be available online.

The system must, on demand through a cataloging terminal, produce a printed listing of the authority files.

The system must have the future capability of "blanket" changes to authority files (e.g., change all subject occurrences of aeroplanes to airplanes).

APPENDIX D / MISCELLANEOUS SPECIFICATIONS

Data Base

The circulation system data base will consist of a file
of bibiliographic records in full MARC II format as
implemented by OCLC. The data base will also contain
records for materials for which MARC formats have not
been implemented.

The initial data base will be created by loading tapes
of bibliographic records from the machine readable data
base. Regular updates to the circulation data base
will be made routinely. The circulation system must be
able to read these tapes and load data from them.
_____ tapes are produced in the MARC II format
with the local call number in the 984 field. The
system must use the bibliographic data on the tape to
create the bibliographic record and the local call
number to create the item record.

The proposed system should provide some automatic method
to facilitate maintenance of the circulation data base
using either _____ update tapes or interface
directly with a _____ in-house OCLC terminal. Each
vendor must describe in the proposal how the system
facilitates data base maintenance using both _____
update tapes and interface with _____'s OCLC
terminal.

Will the data base be partitioned in order to identify
duplicates? If not, how will duplicate identification
be accomplished? How does the data base differentiate
between duplicates and new editions?

_____ will not have its catalogs completely
converted to machine-readable form when the circulation
system is installed. Consequently, the initial data
base will not have bibliographic records for all items
in the collection. It must be possible, for items that
are presented for charge which are not represented in
the data base, to enter a temporary brief bibliographic
record for circulation purposes.

The system must collect circulation statistics for
items circulated on temporary brief bibliographic
records.

Temporary brief bibliographic records must be automatically deleted by the system when the item is discharged.

The system must provide for a permanent brief bibliographic record to be used for certain types of material, such as paperback books. The system must treat these permanent records as if they were full bibliographic records.

The system must be able to generate overdue notices and assess fines for items circulated on temporary brief bibliograpic records.

It must be possible to enter bibliographic records directly into the circulation data base via keyboard from designated terminals.

It must be possible to transfer bibliographic records and other data from the _____ data base to the circulation data base via an online interface between the two systems.

It must be possible to display in its entirety, on designated terminals, any bibliographic record in the database including MARC tags, to edit selectively any record, and to replace the original record with the altered record. It must be possible to delete the entire record, _except_ that the system must not allow a bibliographic record to be deleted as long as there are any item records attached to it. The ability to edit or delete bibliographic records must be limited by password to authorized staff and must be limited to designated terminals.

Item records will be completed via keyboard by library staff at _____ headquarters.

It must be possible to display in its entirety any borrower record on designated terminals, to edit selectively any field in the record without having to re-enter the entire record, and to replace the original record with the altered record. It must be possible to delete the entire record. The ability to edit or delete borrower records must be limited to authorized staff by password.

The system must store individual _____ library call numbers in the item record.

APPENDIX E

Examples of Contract Specifications

(MV)   <u>Mandatory, Verbatim</u> - To be considered responsive, the vendor must agree to execute a contract(s) that includes the provision exactly as written; except that where equivalent alternative language has previously been accepted by ___ and is currently contained in a contract competively awarded to the vendor by ___, such alternative language may, at the sole option of ___, be accepted.

(MC)   <u>Mandatory, Content</u> - To be considered, the vendor must agree to execute a contract(s) that includes language addressing the general intent of the provision as written. For requirements coded MC, vendor proposals must include the specific contract language offered to ___ or indicated verbatim acceptance of ___'s language, if appropriate.

TO BE ADJUDGED RESPONSIVE TO THIS RFP, VENDORS MUST ANSWER EA H REQUIREMENT SET FORTH IN THE CONTRACT PROVISIONS. FAILURE TO DO SO WILL DISQUALIFY A VENDOR FROM FURTHER CONSIDERATION.

(AGENCY AGREEMENT VERSION)

GENERAL PROVISIONS - MANDATORY VERBATIM

MV   1. Governing Law

MV   2. Severability

MV   3. Waiver

MV 4. Independent Status of Contractor

MV 5. Non-Allocation of Funds

MV 6. Subcontractors

MV 7. Advance Payment

MV 8. Quiet Possession and Usage

MV 9. Limitation of Liability

MV 10. Failure to Perform

MV 11. Save Harmless

(AGENCY AGREEMENT VERSION)

GENERAL PROVISIONS - MANDATORY CONTENT

MC 12. Installation (Site) Security

MC 13. Contractor Commitments, Warranties and Representations

MC 14. Risk of Loss (Lease or Rental)

MC 15. Risk of Loss (Purchased)

MC 16. Maintenance Documentation

MC 17. Title (Purchased)

MC 18. Title (Leased)

MC 19. Relocation (Leased Equipment)

MC 20. Patent and Copyright Indemnification

MC 21. Alterations and Attachments

MC 22. Equipment Condition

MC 23. Software Documentation

MC   24.   Contractor Correction of Software Malfunction

MC   25.   Anti-Trust Violations

(AGENCY AGREEMENT VERSION)

STANDARD PROVISIONS - MANDATORY AS MARKED

MC   26.   Installation and Delivery Dates

MC   27.   Liquidated Damages - General

MC   28.   Liquidated Damages - Installation of Equipment

MC   29.   Liquidated Damages - Delivery of System Control Programs

MC   30.   Liquidated Damages - Delivery of Licensed Programs

MC   31.   Liquidated Damages - Site Preparation

MC   32.   Standard of Performance and Acceptance of Equipment

MC   33.   Maintenance of Equipment

MC   34.   Engineering Changes

1.   Governing Law

     This contract shall be governed in all respects by the Law and statutes of the State of ____. The venue of any action hereunder shall be in the District Court for ____ County, ____.

2.   Severability

     If any term or condition of this contract or the application thereof to any person(s) or circumstances is held invalid, such invalidity shall not affect other terms, conditions or applications which can be given effect without the invalid term, condition or application; to this end the terms and conditions of this contract are declared severable.

3. Waiver

Waiver of any breach of any term or condition of this contract shall not be deemed a waiver of any prior or subsequent breach. No term or condition of this contract shall be held to be waived, modified or deleted except by an instrument, in writing, signed by the parties hereto.

4. Independent Status of Contractor

The parties hereto, in the performance of this contract, will be acting in their individual capacities and not as agents, employees, partners, joint venturers or associates of one another. The employees or agents of one party shall not be deemed or construed to be the employees or agents of the other party for any purpose whatsoever.

5. Non-Allocation of Funds

If funds are not allocated for this contract for periodic payment in any future biennial fiscal period, ____ County Board of Directors and ____ Township will not be obligated to pay the net remainder of agreed to consecutive periodic payments remaining unpaid beyond the end of the then-current biennium.
____ agrees to notify the Contractor of such nonallocation at the earliest possible time. No penalty shall accrue to ____ County or ____ Township in the event this provision shall be exercised. This provision shall not be construed so as to permit ____ to terminate this contract in order to acquire similar equipment from a third party.

6. Subcontractors

The Contractor may, with prior written permission from ____, enter into subcontracts with third parties for its performance of any part of the Contractor's duties and obligations, PROVIDED that in no event shall the existence of a subcontract operate to release or reduce the liability of the Contractor to ____ for any breach in the performance of the contractor's duties. The Contractor agrees that all subcontractors shall be agents of the Contractor, and the Contractor agrees to hold the ____ harmless hereunder for any loss or damage of any kind occasioned by the acts or omissions of the Contractor's subcontractors, their agents, or employees.

7.   Advance Payment

No advance payment shall be made for goods or services furnished by Contractor pursuant to this contract.

8.   Quiet Possession and Usage

The ____ upon paying the amounts due hereunder and performing all other convenants, terms, and conditions on its part to be performed hereunder, may and shall peacefully and quietly have, hold, possess, and enjoy the equipment for the term provided without suit, molestation, or interruption.

9.   Limitation of Liability

The parties agree that neither the County nor the Contractor shall be liable to each other, regardless of the form of action, for consequential damages. The parties further agree that neither shall be liable to the other for any lost profits or any demand or claim, regardless of the form of action, against either party by any other person except a claim or demand based on patent or copyright infringement, in which case liability shall be as set forth elsewhere in this contract.

Neither the Contractor nor ____ shall be liable for damages arising from causes beyond the reasonable control and without the fault or negligence of either the Contractor, ____ or their respective subcontractors. Such causes may include, but are not restricted to, acts of God or of the public enemy, acts of any governmental body acting in either its sovereign or contractual capacity, war, explosions, fires, floods, epidemics, quarantine restrictions, strikes, freight embargoes, and unusually severe weather; but in every case the delays must be beyond the reasonable control and without fault or negligence of the Contractor, ____, or their respective subcontractors. If delays are caused by the default of a subcontractor without its fault or negligence, neither the Contractor nor ____ shall be liable for damages for delays, unless the supplies or services to be furnished by their subcontractors were obtainable on comparable terms from other sources in sufficient time to permit the Contractor or ____ to meet its required performance schedule.

Neither party shall be liable for personal injury or damage to tangible property except personal injury or damage to tangible property proximately caused by each party's respective fault or negligence.

10. Failure to Perform

In the event Contractor has failed to perform a substantial obligation to be performed by the Contractor under this agreement and 30 days after written notice of said failure to perform is provided to Contractor said failure has not been cured, then ____ may withhold all monies due and payable including losses and expenses to Contractor, without penalty, until such failure to perform is cured or otherwise adjudicated.

11. Save Harmless

Contractor shall protect, indemnify and save the ____ harmless from and against any damage, cost or liability including reasonable attorney's fees, for any or all injuries to persons or tangible property arising from acts or omissions of Contractor, its officers, employees, agents, or subcontractors howsoever caused.

12. Installation (Site) Security

Contractor, its agents, employees or subcontractors shall conform in all respects with physical, fire or other published security regulations while on the ___'s premises.

13. Contractor Commitments, Warranties and Representations

Any written commitment by the Contractor within the scope of this contract shall be binding upon the Contractor. Failure of the Contractor to fulfill such a commitment shall render the Contractor liable for liquidated or other damages due the ____ under the terms of this contract.

For purposes of this contract, a commitment by the Contractor, which must be in writing, includes: (1) prices and options committed to remain in force over a specified period(s) of time; (2) any warranty or representation made by the Contractor in a proposal as to hardware or software performance or any other physical, design or functional characteristics of a machine, software package or system; (3) any warranty or representation made by a Contractor concerning the characteristics or items in (2) above, contained in any literature, descriptions, drawings or specifications accompanying or referred to in a proposal; (4) any modification of or affirmation or representation as to the above which is made by Contractor in writing in or during the course of negotiation whether or not incorporated into a formal amendment to the proposal in question; and (5) any representation by a Contractor in a proposal, supporting documents or negotiations subsequent thereto as to training to be provided, services to be performed, prices and options committed to remain in force over a fixed period of time or any other similar matter regardless of the fact that the duration of such commitment may exceed the duration of this Contract.

14. Risk of Loss (Lease or Rental)

During the period the machines, model changes, or features are in transit or in the possession of ____ and until such time as title is accepted by ____, Contractor and its insurers, if any, relieve ____ of responsibility for all risks of loss or damage to the machines, model changes, or features except for responsibility for loss or damage attributable to ____'s fault or negligence.

15. Risk of Loss (Purchased)

During the period the machines, model changes, or features are in transit or in possession of ____, up to and including the date or installation, Contractor and its insurers, if any relieve ____ or responsibility for all risks of loss or damage to the machines, including damage caused by ____'s negligence. After the date of installation, the risk of loss or damage shall be borne by ____ except loss or damage attributable to Contractor's fault or negligence.

16. Maintenance Documentation

For purchased Equipment, Contractor shall upon request, provide to ____ such current diagrams, schematics, manuals, and other documents necessary for the maintenance of the Equipment by ____ or its subcontractor. There shall be no additional charge for said maintenance documents.

17. Title (Purchased)

Upon completion of acceptance testing, the Contractor shall convey to ____ good title to purchased equipment free and clear of all liens, pledges, mortgages, encumbrances, or other security interests, except for any security interest associated with an installment payment agreement between ____ and Contractor.

18. <u>Title (Leased)</u>

Equipment furnished hereunder to which the Contractor retains title shall remain personal property and, except as otherwise provided herein, title thereto is retained by the Contractor. ____ shall do nothing to impair or encumber the Contractor's title or rights nor to remove or obscure the property identification markers of the Contractor. ____ under a lease contract will not be responsible for any tax prohibited by the State of ____. The Contractor shall have the right to inspect the equipment during ____'s normal business hours. For all leased or rented equipment for which the Contractor grants to ____ an option to purchase, the Contractor shall keep said equipment free and clear of all liens or other claims.

19. <u>Relocation (Leased Equipment)</u>

Except in an emergency, equipment rented or leased under this contract shall not be moved from the general location in which installed, unless the contractor has been given 30 days prior written notice that move is to be made. For emergency relocation ____ will provide notification to the Contractor within seven calendar days after such relocation.

20. <u>Patent and Copyright Indemnification</u>

Lease or Rental Equipment.

Contractor will at its expense defend ____ against a claim that machines or programming supplied hereunder infringes a U.S. patent or copyright, or that the machines' operation pursuant to a current release and modification level of any programming supplied by Contractor infringes a U.S. patent. Contractor will pay resulting costs, damages and attorney's fees finally awarded provided that:

a. ____ promptly notifies Contractor in writing of the claim; and

b. Contractor has sole control of the defense and all related settlement negotiations, but to the best interest of ____.

If such claim has occurred, or in Contractor's opinion is likely to occur, ____ agrees to permit Contractor at its option and

194

expense, either to procure for ____ the right to continue using the machines or programming or to replace or modify the same so that they become non-infringing and functionally equivalent. If neither of the foregoing alternatives is reasonably available, ____ agrees to return the machines or programming at Contractor's risk and expense upon written request by Contractor. In the event the product has been installed less than one year, transportation to the initial installation site paid by the Lessee shall be refunded by the Contractor. No termination charges will be payable on such returned machines. Contractor agrees to grant ____ a credit for returned machines as depreciated. The depreciation shall be an equal amount per year over the life of the machines.

For this section only, the depreciation shall be calculated on the basis of a useful life of ten (10) years commencing on the effective date of purchase and shall be an equal amount per year over said useful life. The depreciation for fractional parts of a year shall be prorated on the basis of 365 days per year.

Contractor has no liability for any claim based upon the combination, operation or use of any machines or programming supplied hereunder with equipment not supplied by Contractor, or with any program other than or in addition to programming supplied by Contractor if such claim would have been avoided by use of another program capable of achieving the same results, or based upon alteration of the machines or modification of any programming supplied hereunder, if such claim would have been avoided by the absense of such alteration or modification.

Purchase Equipment.

Contractor will at its expense defend ____ against a claim that machines or programming supplied hereunder infringes a U.S. patent or copyright, or that the machines' operation pursuant to a current release and modification level of any programming supplied by Contractor infringes a U.S. patent. Contractor will pay resulting costs, damages and attorney's fees finally awarded provided that:

a.   ____ promptly notifies Contractor in writing of the claim; and

b.   Contractor has sole control of the defense and all related settlement negotiations but to the best interest of ____.

If such claim has occurred or in Contractor's opinion is likely to occur, ____ agrees to permit Contractor at its option and expense either to procure for the Purchaser the right to continue using the machines or programming or to replace or modify the same so that they become noninfringing and functionally equivalent. If neither of the foregoing alternatives is reasonably available, ____ agrees to return the machines or programming at Contractor's risk and expense upon written request by Contractor. In the event the product has been installed less than one year, transportation to the initial installation site paid by ____ shall be refunded by the Contractor.

Contractor has no liability for any claim based upon the combination, operation or use of any machines or programming supplied hereunder with equipment not supplied by Contractor, or with any program other than or in addition to programming supplied by Contractor, if such claim would have been avoided by use of another program capable of performing the same function or result. Contractor has no liability for any claim based upon alteration of the machines or modification of any programming supplied hereunder, if such claim would have been avoided by the absence of such alteration or modification.

The foregoing states the entire obligation of Contractor with respect to infringement of patents and copyrights.

21. Alterations and Attachments

Alterations in or attachments to leased or rented machines may be made upon prior written consent of Contractor, which consent shall not be unreasonably withheld.

Maintenance credit provisions, as contained in this contract, will not apply if equipment failure is caused by such alterations or attachments not furnished by Contractor and lease, rental or maintenance charges shall continue without interruption.

22. Equipment Condition

Contractor warrants that Equipment acquired subject to the agreement is either newly manufactured from new and serviceable used parts which are equivalent to new in performance, reliability and durability.

23. Software Documentation

Contractor will provide appropriate software documentation, within 30 days after execution of this agreement or as otherwise mutually agreed, in the form of a mutually agreed number of manuals adequate for use of software ordered under the provisions of this agreement. Manual upgrades are provided on a no-charge basis through the contractor's local sales and service office.

For all Contractor programs furnished to ____ within the scope of this agreement, the Contractor agrees that in the event it withdraws its support (if supported) from such programs, it will immediately furnish to ____, if requested, at no additional cost, sufficient documentation to permit the ____ to maintain, modify or enhance such purchased or licensed programs.

Contractor grants to ____ the right to copy or otherwise reproduce manuals and documentation furnished pursuant to this provision, for use within the scope of this agreement at no additional charge.

24. Contractor Correction of Software Malfunction

Contractor shall provide a correction service at no additional cost to ____ for any error, malfunction, or defect, if any, in the Contractor supplied software which, when used as delivered, fails to perform in accordance with Contractor's officially announced technical specifications and which ____ shall bring to Contractor's attention. Contractor shall undertake such correction service in a timely manner and shall use its best efforts to make corrections in a manner which is mutually beneficial.

When Contractor performs services pursuant to this agreement which require the use of ____'s computer system(s), ____ agrees to make it available at reasonable times and in reasonable time increments and in no event will ____ charge the Contractor for such system use.

25. Anti-Trust Violations

Contractor and ____ recognize that in actual economic practice overcharges resulting from antitrust violations are in fact usually borne by the Lessee/Purchaser. Therefore, vendor hereby assigns to ____ any and all claims for such overcharges as to goods and materials purchased in connection with this order or contract, except as to overcharges not passed on to ____ resulting from antitrust violations commencing after the date of

197

the bid, quotation, or other event establishing the price under this order or contract.

26. Installation and Delivery Dates

The Contractor shall install the equipment, ready for use on or before the installation date(s) specified _____. The equipment shall not be considered ready for use until the Contractor provides _____ with documentation of a successful system audit utilizing Contractor's diagnostic routines, performed at _____'s installation site, which demonstrates that the equipment meets minimum design capabilities and after reviewing such documentation _____ agrees that the equipment is ready to begin acceptance testing and so notifies Contractor in writing.

Contractor agrees to provide _____ with written specifications for the installation site within _____ days after the equipment is ordered. _____ agrees to have the equipment installation site prepared in accordance with Contractor's written specifications prior to the facility readiness date specified _____. _____ shall provide the Contractor access to the equipment installation site prior to the installation date for purpose of installing the equipment.

27. Liquidated Damages - General

Any delay by the Contractor to perform will interfere with the proper implementation of _____'s programs to the loss and damage of _____.

Similarly, delay by _____ in readying the facility or permitting installation will interfere with the schedule under which the Contractor is operating, thus resulting in damage to the Contractor.

As it would be impracticable to fix the actual damage sustained in the event of any such failure to perform, _____ and the Contractor, therefore, presume that in the event of any such failure to perform, the amount of damage which will be sustained will be the amount set forth elsewhere in this contract and they agree that the Contractor and _____ shall pay such amount as liquidated damages and not as a penalty.

Amounts due _____ as liquidated damages may be deducted by _____ from any money payable to the Contractor pursuant to this contract or ____ may bill the Contractor as a separate item. ____ shall notify the Contractor in writing of any claim for liquidated damages pursuant to this provision at least 30 days prior to the date ____ deducts such sums from money payable to the Contractor.

Liquidated damages provided for under the terms of this agreement are subject to the same limitations as provided for in Section __ of this contract, "Limitation of Liability."

28. Liquidated Damages - Installation of Equipment

If the Contractor does not install the system and/or machines described in this contract and special features and accessories described in this contract with the system and/or machines, ready for use on or before the installation date set forth _____ the Contractor shall pay to ____ as fixed and agreed liquidated damages in lieu of all other damages due to such noninstallation, for each calendar day between the agreed installation date set forth _____ and the date such equipment is installed ready for use by not more than one-hundred eighty (180) calendar days, an amount of $100 per day, or 1/30th of the basic monthly lease or rental contract charge, whichever is greater, for all equipment regardless of whether said equipment is rented, leased, or purchased.

If some, but not all, of the machines on order are installed, ready for use, by the stipulated installation date, ____ uses any such installed machines, ____ agrees to pay the normal lease rate described in this Agreement for the machines used. If the Contractor provides suitable substitute equipment acceptable to ____ on or before the stipulated installation date, no liquidated damages shall apply to the ordered equipment. When the Contractor provides suitable substitute equipment acceptable to ____, monthly charges shall be the rate for the equipment ordered or the rate for substitute equipment, whichever is less. When a substitute product is replaced with an ordered product, the contracted equipment rate will apply.

Any monthly lease or rental payments made and any purchase option credits accrued for substitute equipment shall be transferred to the ordered product, as if the ordered product had been initially installed.

If the delay is more than 30 calendar days, then by written notice to the Contractor, ____ may terminate the right of the

Contractor to install and may obtain substitute equipment. In this event, the Contractor shall be liable for liquidated damages, in the amounts specified above, until substitute equipment is installed, ready for use, or for 180 days from the installation date, whichever occurs first. The Contractor shall be liable for inbound and outbound preparation and shipping costs for equipment returned pursuant to this provision.

29. Liquidated Damages - Delivery of System Control Programs

If the Contractor does not deliver all the System Control Programs described in Schedule___ attached hereto, ready for operation in substantial conformance with the Contractor's specifications on or before the specified installation dates, ____ may at its option delay the equipment installation date and the Contractor shall pay to ____ as fixed and agreed liquidated damages the amount of one hundred dollars ($100), irrespective of the number of System Control Programs undelivered, for each calendar day between the specified installation dates and the date of the delivery of such System Control Programs, but not for more than 180 calendar days, in lieu of all other damages for nondelivery of programming aids. If the Contractor provides suitable substitution of System Control Programs, acceptable to ____, liquidated damages for nondelivery of System Control Programs shall likewise not apply for any day on which liquidated damages for noninstallation of equipment accrues.

If the Contractor's delay in delivering System Control Programs is more than 30 calendar days, then by written notice to the Contractor, ____ may terminate the right of the Contractor to install or may discontinue the equipment immediately in the event it was already installed. In the event ____ terminates the right of the Contractor to install or ____ discontinues the equipment, the Contractor shall be liable for liquidated damages in the amount of $100, irrespective of the number of System Control Programs undelivered, for each calendar day for a period of time between the installation date and the date that ____ terminates the right of the Contractor to install or the date of discontinuance of the equipment, but not for more than 180 calendar days. The Contractor shall be liable for all inbound and outbound preparation and shipping costs for equipment returned pursuant to this provision.

30. Liquidated Damages - Delivery of Licensed Programs

The shipment dates for licensed programs will be specified

200

in Schedule __. If the Contractor does not ship any of the licensed programs listed on Schedule__ ready for use in substantial accordance with Contractor's official published specifications on or before the specified shipment dates, the contractor shall pay to ____ for each unshipped program fixed and agreed liquidated damages in the amount of 1/30th of the monthly charges or 1/10th of 1% (.001) of the one-time charges if there are no monthly charges up to a maximum of $100 total for all unshipped programs, for each calendar day between the specified shipment date and the date of shipment of such programs, but not to exceed 180 calendar days, in lieu of all other damages. If the Contractor provides suitable substitution of licensed programs accptable to ____ damages shall not apply, provided however, liquidated damages will apply if such substituted licensed programs are shipped later than the specified shipment date.

31. Liquidated Damages - Site Preparation

In the event the equipment installation site is not prepared by the facility readiness date specified _____, ____ shall pay to the Contractor as fixed and agreed liquidated damages, an amount equal to the 1/30th of the basic monthly lease or rental contract charge for all equipment regardless of whether said equipment is rented, leased, or purchased, for each calendar day between the specified facility readiness date and the actual readiness date, but not to exceed 180 calendar days in lieu of all other damages. The charges for any 30-day period shall not exceed the basic monthly lease or rental contract charge.

In the event a change directed by ____ requires a later installation date of certain equipment and ____ has failed to notify the Contractor of the delay on or before the change notification date specified _____, ____ shall pay the Contractor an amount equal to 1/30th of the basic monthly lease or rental contract charge of said equipment, for each day between the scheduled installation date and the new installation date, but not to exceed 180 calendar days in lieu of all other damages. The charges for any 30-day period shall not exceed the basic monthly contract charge.

____ shall not be liable for liquidated damages under both paragraphs above during the same period of time with respect to the same equipment.

32. Standard of Performance and Acceptance of Equipment

This provision establishes a standard of performance which must be met before any of the Equipment is accepted by ____. It is also applicable to any replacement or substitute machines and machines which are added, or field modified after completion of a successful Performance Period.

The Performance Period shall begin when the Equipment is installed and ready for use and shall end when the Equipment has met the Standard of Performance for a period of 30 consecutive days by operating in conformance with the Contractors technical speci-ications (or as quoted in any proposal) and at an effectiveness level of at least 95 percent.

In the event the Equipment does not meet the Standard of Performance during the initial 30 consecutive days the Standard of Performance test shall continue on a day-to-day basis until the Standard of Performance is met for a total of 30 consecutive days. If the Equipment fails to meet the Standard of Performance after 90 calendar days, from commencement of Acceptance Testing, ____ may, at its option, either terminate the Equipment without penalty, request replacement equipment, or continue the performance test. The Contractor shall be liable for all inbound and outbound preparation and shipping costs for equipment returned pursuant to this provision. The ____'s option to terminate the Equipment Order under this Agreement shall remain in effect until such time as a successful completion of the performance period is attained.

(Lease Only) - Lease and maintenance charges shall apply beginning on the first day of the successful performance period.

The effectiveness level for a machine is a percentage figure determined by dividing the operational use time of the machine by the sum of that time plus machine failure downtime.

Operational use time for performance testing for a machine is defined as the accumulated time during which the machine is in actual use.

Machine failure downtime is that period of time when scheduled jobs cannot be processed on that machine due to machine or Contractor supplied software malfunction.

Contractor supplied software shall, for purposes of this Agreement, mean library software packages released and generally offered to lessees or purchasers of Contractor's Equipment as modified and offered by Contractor from time to time as library software.

During periods of machine downtime, ____ may use operable equipment when such action does not interfere with maintenance of the inoperable equipment.

Machine failure downtime for added, field modified, substitute, or replacement machines after the completion of a successful Performance Period is that period of time when such machines are inoperable due to machine or Contractor supplied software malfunction.

Downtime for each incident shall start from the time ____ makes a bona fide attempt to contact the Contractor's designated representative at the prearranged contact point until the machine(s) is returned to ____ in proper operating condition, exclusive of either contracted response time agreed to by the Contractor and ____ or actual response time, whichever is less.

During the performance period for a machine a minimum of 100 hours of operational use time with productive or simulated work will be required as a basis for computation of the effectiveness level. However, in computing the effectiveness level the actual number of operational use hours shall be used when in excess of the minimum of 100 hours.

____ shall maintain appropriate daily records to satisfy the requirements of this provision and shall notify the Contractor in writing of the date of the first day of the successful Performance Period.

Equipment shall not be accepted and no charges shall be paid until the Standard of Performance is met. The date of acceptance shall be the first day of the successful Performance Period.

Operational use time and downtime shall be measured in hours and whole minutes.

31.   Maintenance of Equipment

Contractor agrees to maintain the Equipment to original performance specifications and in accordance with the following maintenance terms and conditions during the term, or extension thereof, of any lease entered into pursuant to this Agreement.

Contractor further agrees that, for purchased Equipment, Contractor will, at the sole option of the Purchaser, maintain the Equipment to original performance specifications and in accordance with the following maintenance terms and conditions for a period of five (5) years from date of acceptance of any Equipment purchased pursuant to this agreement, provided that said Equipment has been continuously maintained by the Contractor, or the Contractor's authorized Sub-contractor, since its acceptance. Maintenance for purchased Equipment may be discontinued by the Purchaser upon ninety (90) days written notice to Contractor.

Maintenance charges are as set forth on Schedules __ and __.

A. General Provisions

(1) ____ shall provide the Contractor access to the equipment to perform maintenance service.

(2) Preventive maintenance shall be performed at a time convenient to ____ within or contiguous with contracted periods of maintenance. The Contractor shall specify in writing, for each machine, the number of hours it requires per month for preventive maintenance and the frequency and duration of such preventive maintenance. From this Contractor supplied information ____ shall develop and provide to the Contractor in writing the schedule within which the Contractor shall provide preventive maintenance. This schedule may be modified by mutual agreement.

(3) Remedial maintenance shall be performed after notification that Equipment is inoperative. The Contractor shall provide ____ with a designated point of contact and shall make arrangements to enable the maintenance representative to receive such notification.

(4) Contracted response time is defined as the time, as specified on the ADP Equipment Order, within which Contractor's maintenance personnel must arrive at ____'s Equipment installation site after notification by ____ that maintenance service is required.

(5)   Except for causes beyond the control of the
      Contractor, if the maintenance personnel fail to
      arrive at ____'s installation site within the
      contracted response period, the Contractor shall
      grant a credit to ____ in the amount of 1/200th of
      the basic monthly lease and maintenance charges
      for each "late" hour or part thereof (prorated)
      beginning with the time of notification and ending
      with the time of arrival. For purpose of response
      time computations, only hours of contracted
      maintenance shall be included; except that, of any
      portion of the Contracted Response Time falls
      outside contracted periods of maintenance, the
      maintenance personnel shall arrive at the
      beginning of the following period of contracted
      maintenance.

(6)   The Contractor shall furnish a malfunction
      incident report to the installation upon
      completion of each maintenance call. The report
      shall include, as a minimum, the following:

      (a)   Date and time notified;
      (b)   Date and time of arrival;
      (c)   Type and Serial Number(s) of machine(s);
      (d)   Time spent for repair;
      (e)   Description of malfunction;
      (f)   List of parts replaced;
      (g)   Additional charges, if applicable.

(7)   There shall be no additional charges for
      replacement parts.

(8)   Maintenance Credit for Equipment Malfunction

      (a) If a machine remains inoperative due to a
      malfunction through no fault or negligence of ____
      for a total of 12 hours or more during any 24-hour
      period, the Contractor shall grant a credit to
      ____ for each such hour in the amount of 1/200th
      of the basic monthly lease and maintenance charges
      for any machine not usable as a result of the
      breakdown; provided that, for equipment supplied
      by other vendors, the credit shall be as mutually
      agreed. Downtime for each incident shall start

from the time _____ makes a bona fide attempt to contact the Contractor's designated representative at the prearranged contact point and continue until the machine is returned in good operating condition; PROVIDED THAT, time required, as a result of the malfunction to reconstruct data stored on disks and/or other storage media, shall be considered down time for that equipment required for said reconstruction; and PROVIDED FURTHER THAT, outside primary service areas specified on Schedule __, downtime for each incident shall be reduced by either the contracted response time or the actual response time whichever is less.

When maintenance credit is due the total number of creditable hours shall be accumulated for the month and adjusted to the nearest half hour.

(b)   Exclusive of the provisions of Paragraph __ above, the Contractor shall grant a credit to _____ for any machine being maintained by the Contractor which fails to perform at an effectiveness level of 98 percent during any month. The effectiveness level for a machine is computed by dividing the operational use time by the sum of that time plus machine failure downtime.

Downtime shall be defined and computed in the same manner as provided in subparagraph __ above. The credit shall be a reduction of the total monthly lease and maintenance charges by the percentage figure determined by subtracting the actual effectiveness level percentage from 95 percent. For example, if the effectiveness level for a machine is 82 percent, the credit would be 13 percent. Any downtime for which credit was granted in accordance with Paragraph __ above shall not be included in the effectiveness level computation.

(c)   In the event that a leased machine, or a purchased machine which has been installed less than two years, is inoperative due to machine failure and the total number of hours of downtime exceeds ten per cent (10%) of the total operations use time for three consecutive calendar months, ____ reserves the right to require the Contractor to replace the machine. The purchase option and/or age depreciation credits for the replacement machines shall not be less than the credits accrued from the date of installation of the original machine, regardless of whether the replacement is made at the request of ____ or for the convenience of the Contractor.

(9) There shall be no additional maintenance charges for:

(a) Preventive maintenance, regardless of when performed.

(b) Remedial maintenance which was begun during the principal period of maintenance or extension thereof or when the Contractor was notified during the principal period of maintenance or extension thereof of the need for remedial maintenance.

(c) Remedial maintenance required within a 48-hour period due to recurrence of the same malfunction.

(d) Time spent by maintenance personnel after arrival at the site awaiting the arrival of additional maintenance personnel and/or delivery of parts, tools or other required material after a service call has commenced.

(e) Remedial maintenance required when the scheduled preventive maintenance preceding the malfunction had not been performed.

(10) Malfunctioning equipment must be repaired or a replacement spare installed by the Contractor's maintenance technician no later than the close of business on the work day following notification of equipment malfunction. Failure of the contractor to comply with this requirement shall be a failure to perform.

B. "On-Call" Maintenance

(1) The basic monthly maintenance charges set forth in Schedules __ shall entitle ____ to maintenance service during a principal period of maintenance.

(2) ____ by giving fifteen (15) days written notice to the Contractor, may extend the principal period of maintenance in the time increments, and for the charges as shown in Schedule__.

(3) The principal period of maintenance service outside the designated principal period of maintenance or extension thereof on an on-call basis, charges for such additional maintenance service shall be as shown in Schedule __. Only one maintenance person shall respond to a request for maintenance unless it is mutually agreed that more than one person is required.

C. Replacement Parts

Contractor shall furnish replacement parts for the equipment for a period of seven (7) years commencing with the date(s) of acceptance of the equipment in accordance with acceptance criteria elsewhere in this Contract. After the expiration of said seven (7) year period, Contractor, when requested by ____ shall furnish all data necessary to enable ____ to purchase such replacement parts or have them manufactured elsewhere.

34. Engineering Changes

Contractor warrants that installation of such engineering changes as Contractor may from time to time require or recommend shall not cause the performance of the machine modified to be materially degraded below the Contractor's official published specifications at the time of installation of the equipment. If such engineering changes are scheduled to take 2 hours or less, they shall be installed at a mutually agreeable time during contracted hours of maintenance. Engineering changes scheduled to take in excess of two hours shall be installed at a mutually agreeable time.

EXHIBIT 1 - SAMPLE CONTRACT

AGREEMENT FOR THE PURCHASE AND SALE OF
DATA PROCESSING EQUIPMENT AND
THE LICENSE OF SOFTWARE

This Agreement, dated as of _____, by and between
_____ ("Contractor") and _____("Buyer")
for the purchase and sale of the Equipment and Software which
comprise the _____described in detail herein, which
shall be installed at _____ referred to herein as
"Buyer"), and those remote sites specified herein.

1. Exhibits and References.
(a) Incorporation of Exhibits. The Contractor and the
Buyer agree that the following documents are incorporated into
this Agreement as if set forth in their entirety herein. In the
event of any conflicts among the provisions of such documents,
the lowered numbered Exhibits shall control over the higher
numbered Exhibits, provided, however, that this Agreement shall
take precedence over all Exhibits.

1. REQUEST FOR PROPOSALS for an AUTOMATED ON-LINE
    CIRCULATION CONTROL SYSTEM for
    _____ dated _____ revised
    _____ and_____ and_____
    ("RFP") as Exhibit 1.

2. PROPOSAL for an AUTOMATED CIRCULATION CONTROL
    SYSTEM for _____ dated
    _____("Proposal") as Exhibit 2.

3. Site Preparation Requirements Manual
    dated _____ as Exhibit 3.

4. CIRCULATION CONTROL REFERENCE MANUAL dated
    _____ as Exhibit 4.

Contractor and Buyer hereby reference and include as
Exhibits 5 and 6, respectively, to this Agreement the following
documents:

5. Maintenance Agreement by and between Contractor and
    Buyer dated of even date herewith as Exhibit 5.

6. Escrow Agreement by and between Cont actor and Buyer dated of even date herewith as Exhibit 6.

(b) Ronerences. The Contractor and the Buyer agree further that for ease of reference certain portions of the RFP have been referenced expressly herein. Such references are solely for the convenience of the parties and are not intended to designate any hierarchy of importance of the provisions of the RFP.

2. Purchase of Equipment and License of Software.
The Buyer hereby agrees to purchase and Contractor hereby agrees to sell the equipment listed on RFP Exhibit A, pages 9A, 9B and 9C of Exhibit 1 hereto (collectively the "Equipment"), and Contractor agrees to grant a license for the use of the computer programs and related documentation listed on RFP Exhibit A, pages 9A, 9B and 9C of Exhibit 1 hereto (collectively the "Software"), at the price specified on RFP Exhibit A, pages 9A, 9B and 9C of Exhibit 1 hereto (the "Purchase Price"), upon the terms and conditions set forth in this Agreement. The Equipment and the Software are sometimes collectively referred to herein as the "System."

3. Site Preparation.
Buyer shall prepare the site for the installation of the Equipment in accordance with RFP Section 5.11.4, of Exhibit 1 hereto, RFP-MC Number 21, of Exhibit 1 hereto, and in compliance with the requirements set forth in Exhibit 3 hereto.

4. Installation (Site) Security.
Contractor, its agents, employees or subcontractors shall conform in all respects with physical, fire or other published security regulations while on the Buyer's premises.

5. Inside Delivery and Installation.
Contractor shall be responsible for the inside delivery and installation of the Equipment and shall connect the same to the power sources which are installed by the Buyer pursuant to Paragraph 3 above. Installation shall be performed during normal business hours, and the Buyer shall make all the necessary arrangements to allow Contractor personnel sufficient work space and access to the installation location(s) during normal business hours or at such other times as may be mutually agreed upon. Where applicable, Contractor shall connect the Equipment to telephone company supplied lines; however, Contractor shall be in no way responsible for the installation, the installation schedule, or the reliability of such telephone company supplied lines. Contractor

shall not be responsible for interfacing the System with any other equipment not purchased from Contractor, without prior written consent of Contractor.

6. License of Software.
(a) License and Term. Subject to the terms and conditions hereinafter set forth, Contractor hereby grants to Buyer a non-transferable, non-exclusive and royalty-free license (the "License") to use the Software solely in the conduct of Buyer's business. Buyer acknowledges that by virtue of this License, Buyer acquires only the right to use the original and permitted duplicate copies of the Software as described herein and does not acquire any rights of ownership in the Software, which rights shall remain exclusively with Contractor. The term of the License shall commence upon delivery of the first module of Software and shall remain in force as long as Buyer is in compliance with all the provisions of this Agreement.

(b) Confidentiality of Software. Buyer agrees that the Software, together with all materials and knowledge related thereto obtained by Buyer, shall be held in confidence and shall not at any time, either during the term of the License or thereafter be made available in any form to any person or entity other than to employees of Buyer to the extent that such disclosure is reasonably necessary to Buyer's use of the Software authorized hereunder, without the express written consent of Contractor.

(c) Permission to Copy Software and Related Materials. Buyer agrees that it will not copy or in any way duplicate Software or any materials related thereto, in whole or in part, except as expressly authorized to do so by this License or by written consent of Contractor. Contractor hereby expressly authorizes Buyer to copy Software for its own use, solely for archive or emergency restart purposes or to replace worn copy.

(d) Materials developed by Contractor or Buyer. Buyer agrees that all training and procedural materials developed by Contractor in conjunction with the Software shall be the property of Contractor. Buyer further agrees that additions and supplements to the Software which may be developed for Buyer through the reimbursed or unreimbursed efforts of Contractor employees or agents, whether or not in conjunction with Buyer's employees or agents, shall be the exclusive property of Contractor.

7. Installation and Delivery Dates.
The provision with respect to installation and delivery dates is set forth at RFP-MC Number 21, pages 79 and 80 of Exhibit 1 hereto.

8.   Documentation.
Contractor will provide Software documentation in accordance with RFP-MC Number 18, page 78 of Exhibit 1 hereto, and in addition:
Contractor agrees to provide Buyer without additional charge, (a) three (3) copies of each Reference Manual for each Software Module purchased under this Agreement, (b) that number of copies of the Contractor Circulation Control Operator's Guide, equal to the number of circulation stations purchased under this Agreement, and (c) that number of copies of the appropriate Training/Operating Manuals, equal to the number of terminals purchased under this Agreement. Contractor has placed a copy of the Software documentation in escrow with _____ Company, a Company having its principal place of business in _____ and Contractor has agreed to designate Buyer as a potential recipient of such Software documentation pursuant to the terms of Exhibit 6 hereto.

9.   Training.
In accordance with the provisions of RFP Sections 2.5.1 and 2.5.2, page 21 of Exhibit 1 hereto, Contractor shall provide, without additional charge, group training sessions on the operation and use of the System for Buyer's personnel. Such sessions will be conducted at the Buyer's site for a total of 10 days prior to and after installation of the System at times to be agreed upon by Contractor and the Buyer. Any additional training required as a result of hardware and/or Software upgrades to the System purchased under this Agreement will be provided as needed, without additional charge, at times to be determined by Contractor and the Buyer. The Buyer shall be responsible for the salaries and the travel expenses of its personnel.

10. Title and Security Interest.
Contractor shall convey to Buyer good title to the Equipment free and clear of all liens, pledges, mortgages and encumbrances. Title to the Equipment shall pass from Contractor to the Buyer upon inside delivery of the Equipment. The Buyer hereby grants to Contractor a purchase money security interest in the Equipment and the proceeds thereof to secure the performance of the Buyer's obligation to pay the Purchase Price hereunder. The security interest shall terminate upon payment by the Buyer to Contractor of the Purchase Price. The Buyer agrees to execute such further documents, financing statement, and other instruments as may be requested by Contractor in order to perfect the security interest granted to it hereby. Contractor agrees to execute and deliver to

212

Buyer a termination statement and such other documentation as may reasonably be requested by Buyer upon completion of such payment.

11. **Proprietary Rights.**
Contractor retains for itself, and the Buyer acknowledges that Contractor so retains, all proprietary rights in and to all designs, engineering details, and other data pertaining to the System, and retains for itself the sole right to manufacture, lease, and sell any and all such systems. The Software and the configuration of the Equipment shall be deemed to be trade secrets of Contractor.

12. **System Modifications.**
Contractor shall provide and install without additional charge to the Buyer (a) such modifications of the construction and/or the design of the Equipment as Contractor shall make available without additional charge to other buyers and (b) all future modifications of the construction and/or the design of the Software. The Buyer shall allow Contractor personnel access to the System during normal business hours, or at such other times as may be mutually agreed upon, for the purpose of installing such modifications. In the event that Contractor provides such modifications to the Buyer, Contractor shall supply documentation and training which shall be sufficient for the use and operation of the System by the Buyer at no additional charge to Buyer.

13. **Terms of Payment.**
The terms of payment under this Agreement are set forth in RFP Section 2.3.7, of Exhibit 1 hereto and invoices will be paid as set forth in RFP Exhibit F, of Exhibit 1 hereto.

14. **Prices.**
Prices are F.O.B. _____. All freight, delivery, and insurance charges will be billed separately and shall be payable by the Buyer upon receipt. Prices do not include any local, state, federal or foreign taxes, tariffs, and duties, if any, which shall be the sole responsibility of the Buyer.

15. **Buyer Responsibilities.**
(a) The Buyer will provide adequate and timely support or information with regard to its administrative, operational and management procedures, and any data necessary to effectively complete implementation or installation of the System.
(b) The Buyer agrees to provide Contractor with certain data that will be incorporated into the building of various data files and

213

which are essential to the implementation of the System. Contractor
will not assume liability for incorrect System performance
resulting from failure of the Buyer to submit appropriate data,
from the submission of erroneous data, or from the Buyer's
administrative, operational or management procedures.

(c) The Buyer shall not attach any device to the System
which has not been purchased from Contractor without the express
written permission from Contractor. If permission is granted, the
Buyer understands that Contractor bears no responsibility for the
performance of the System when used with such a device, nor for
the operation, functional performance, and maintenance of such
devices.

16.   System Acceptance.
The provision with respect to System Acceptance is set forth
in RFP-MC Number 26, of Exhibit 1 hereto.

17.   Warranties and Representations.
(a) Merchantability and Fitness for Purpose. Contractor warrants
that the System will be merchantable and fit for the purpose of
Automated Library Circulation Control, as detailed in Exhibit 1
hereto.

(b) Defects in Material and Workmanship. Contractor warrants the
Equipment against defects in material and workmanship under
normal use and service for a period of one (1) year after
installation and acceptance which shall be determined in
accordance with RFP Section 2.4.4, of Exhibit 1 hereto.
During the one (1) year Equipment Warranty, Contractor and the Buyer
shall perform in accordance with the conditions of the
Maintenance Agreement. Contractor warrants the Software against
defects in material and workmanship under normal use and service
for a period of ninety (90) days from the date of installation
and completion of Full Load Acceptance Test, provided that Buyer
shall have continuously performed its obligations under the
Maintenance Agreement. Contractor's obligations under these warranties
shall be to repair or replace at the Buyer's site, at Contractor's
option, defective parts or programs before the end of the
warranty periods. Failure to make such repairs or replacements
shall extend the warranty periods until such repairs or
replacements are made.

(c) THE WARRANTIES SET FORTH IN THIS ARTICLE 17 ARE IN LIEU
OF ALL IMPLIED WARRANTIES, INCLUDING THE IMPLIED WARRANTIES OF
MERCHANTABILITY OR FITNESS FOR A PARTICULAR PURPOSE.

18.   Limitation of Liability.
The limitation of liability provision is set forth in RFP-MV

Number 8, 75 of Exhibit 1 hereto.

19. <u>Non-Assignability.</u>
Neither party will assign any of its rights or obligations under this Agreement without prior written consent of the other party.

20. <u>Patent and Copyright Indemnification.</u>
Contractor will (1) assume the defense of any suit brought against the Buyer for infringement of any United States patent or copyright arising from use and/or sale of the Equipment or Software under this Agreement, (2) defray the expense, including costs and attorneys' fees, of such defense, and (3) indemnify the Buyer against any monetary damages and/or costs awarded in such suit; provided (1) that Contractor is given sole and exclusive control of the defense of such suit and sole and exclusive control of all negotiations relative to the settlement thereof, (2) that the liability claimed shall have arisen solely because of Contractor's selection as to the design or composition of the Software or the Equipment and that the Software or the Equipment is used by the Buyer in the form, state or condition as delivered by Contractor, (3) that the Buyer shall have performed all of its obligations under this Agreement, and (4) that the Buyer promptly provide Contractor with written notice of any claim with respect to which the Buyer asserts that Contractor assumes responsibility under this Section 20. This Section 20 states the entire liability of Contractor for patent or copyright infringement by the Software or the Equipment or any portions thereof.

21. <u>Governing Law.</u>
This Agreement shall be governed in all respects by the law and statutes of the State of _____ without giving effect to conflicts of law principles.

22. <u>Severability.</u>
The severability provision is set forth at RFP-MV Number 2, page 74 of Exhibit 1 hereto.

23. <u>Waiver.</u>
The waiver provision is set forth at RFP-MV Number 3, page 74 of Exhibit 1 hereto.

24. <u>Independent Status of Contractor.</u>
The independent status of contractor provision is set forth at RFP-MV Number 4, page 74 of Exhibit 1 hereto.

25. Subcontractors.
The subcontractors provision is set forth at RFP-MV Number 6, page 74 of Exhibit 1 hereto.

26. Failure to Perform.
The failure to perform provision is set forth at RFP-MV Number 9, page 76 of Exhibit 1 hereto.

27. Save Harmless.
The save harmless provision is set forth at RFP-MV Number 10, page 76 of Exhibit 1 hereto.

28. Contractor Commitments, Warranties, and Representations.
The provision with respect ot Contractor commitments, warranties, and representations is set forth at RFP-MV Number 12, page 76 of Exhibit 1 hereto.

29. Risk of Loss.
During the period the machines, model changes, or features are in transit or in possession of Buyer, up to and including the date of inside delivery, Contractor and its insurers, if any, relieve Buyer of responsibility for all risks of loss including damage caused by Buyer's negligence. After the date of inside delivery, the risk of loss or damage shall be borne by Buyer except loss or damage attributable to Contractor's fault or negligence.

30. Maintenance Documentation.
The maintenance documentation provision is set forth at RFP-MC Number 14, page 77 of Exhibit 1 hereto.

31. Anti-Trust Violations.
The Anti-Trust provision is set forth at RFP-MC Number 20, page 79 of Exhibit 1 hereto.

32. Engineering Changes.
The engineering changes provision is set forth at RFP-MC Number 28, page 87 of Exhibit 1 hereto.

33. Non-Discrimination.
The non-discrimination provision is set forth at RFP-MC Number 29, page 87 of Exhibit 1 hereto.

34. Insurance.
The insurance provision is set forth at RFP-MV Number 30,

page 88 of Exhibit 1 hereto.

35. __System Maintenance__
Contractor shall maintain the System purchased hereunder in accordance with Exhibit 5 hereof.

36. __Purchase of Additional Equipment and License of Additional Software under this Agreement.__
The Buyer, with the express written agreement of Contractor, has an option to purchase additional equipment and the license of additional software not listed on RFP Exhibit A, pages 9A, 9B and 9C of Exhibit 1 hereto, under the same terms and conditions set forth herein.

37. __Entire Agreement.__
This Agreement including Exhibits 1, 2, 3, 4, 5 and 6 hereto, contains the entire understanding of the parties hereto and neither it nor the rights and obligations hereunder may be changed, modified or waived except by an instrument in writing signed by the parties.

By:_____   By:_____
   Name   Name

   _____   _____
   Title   Title

   _____   _____
   Date   Date

DATE DUE

FE 17 '92					